TROUT
TALK

Other Books by Lesley Crawford:

The Trout Fisher's Handbook, Swan Hill Press 2002

Scotland's Classic Wild Trout Waters, Swan Hill Press 2000

Fishing for Wild Trout in Scottish Lochs, Swan Hill Press 1996

An Angler's Year in Caithness & Sutherland, Northern Times 1992

Caithness & Sutherland, Trout Loch Country, North of Scotland Newspapers 1991

TROUT
TALK

AN A TO Z OF TROUT FISHING

LESLEY CRAWFORD

SWAN·HILL
PRESS

All photography by Lesley Crawford

First published in the UK in 2004
by Swan Hill Press, an imprint of Quiller Publishing Ltd

British Library Cataloguing-in-Publication Data
  A catalogue record for this book
  is available from the British Library

ISBN 1 904057 37 3

The information in this book is true and complete to the best of our knowledge.
All recommendations are made without any guarantee on the part of the
Publisher, who also disclaims any liability incurred in connection with the use of
this data or specific details.

Printed in China

Swan Hill Press

An imprint of Quiller Publishing Ltd.
Wykey House, Wykey, Shrewsbury, SY4 1JA
Tel: 01939 261616 Fax: 01939 261606
E-mail: info@quillerbooks.com
Website: www.swanhillbooks.com

DEDICATION
To dearest Mum 1918–2003
Always in my heart

ACKNOWLEDGEMENTS

I would like to thank the following for their kind assistance in researching this book:

Ann and Ted Bounds, Ron Crawford, Misako Ishimura, Andrew Johnston.

CONTENTS

Introduction 9
A – Z of fishing talk and terms 11
Select Bibliography 189
Index 190

INTRODUCTION

Trout fishermen speak their own language. Whether it is over a cold beer, a long lingering dinner or simply out on the river bank the conversation will be of only one thing, angling. We band of brothers and sisters are held together by this wonderful bond of communication, we simply love to talk about trout fishing in all its shapes and forms. To outsiders it's a complete mystery why the heads of Kings and Commoners will bend together in deep conversation over how to twitch a Daddy, dress a Clouser or cast a Klinkhamer. It's no secret to us though. Rarely do we not unite in the joyful aim of explaining how we tried to catch a trout, what he rose to and how the battle was won or lost. The chat usually flows like good wine no matter your background or creed.

During the writing of my last book *The Trout Fisher's Handbook* it came to me that the vocabulary surrounding trout and trout fishing has expanded almost out of recognition since I began this sport in 1960. For example, gone forever are the days of plain old rod, reel, line and flies. Now we have high modulus graphite, large arbors, Hi Vis Flies and enough variations in fly patterns to kit out a world army. Then there are all those dinky little names we give our clothing, boots, fly tying materials, methods, tactics, even our fish. A visit to America in 2002 opened up yet more angling colloquialisms, some familiar some alien, and the idea for this book was spawned on the redds of conversation.

Trout Talk is therefore the result of extensive, loving research. It attempts to bring a whole melange of British and American trout fishing terminology back home under one roof. Let it expand your knowledge, widen your angling horizons and maybe bring on a smile or two for ultimately trout fishing should be good fun, pure and simple…

Lesley Crawford 2004

Abundance Factor

While trout are opportunistic feeders they also like an easy life and prefer to latch on to the most abundant source of food located in their territory. Whatever is most profuse at the time they will have a go at, be that midge, mayfly or crustaceans. Next time you are out on river or lake watch how trout come on the feed as the hatch goes from a trickle to a flood. It is just as if someone has pulled a switch. This is the Abundance Factor at its best and it's high time you got your fly on the water.

Ace of Spades

This is an English reservoir trout fly originally designed as a *lure* for rainbow trout but just as useful for deeper water brown trout fishing especially early in the season. Tied with black Matuka style wings (Americans would call it *streamer* style) and fished on a slow *retrieve* on intermediate or sinking line this is one of the best 'rainbow' patterns to make a cross over into wild trout fishing. The original dressing by Dave Collyer of England had an overwing of dark bronze mallard or ginger goat hair but if you haven't got these, all black dressings still work well. Don't be tempted to use deer hair as a substitute for mallard or goat, it's too buoyant and turns it into a *Muddler*. Tie on size 6 to 10 longshank hooks.

Acid Rain

Over the years the controversy over acid rain and its potential to pollute freshwater systems has shown little sign of diminishing. Trying to get countries to cut down on harmful sulphur oxide and nitrogen oxide emissions which once in the atmosphere fall back down on us as toxic rain, has been an uphill task. Waters seriously affected by acid rain show little or no aquatic life present and once damaged may take many years to recover if at all. Some Scandinavian waters have been severely affected. Of course we anglers can simply put our heads down and ignore it especially if our particular home waters are unaffected by this type of pollution. However I think we should try to see past the end of our rods and attempt savings on our energy emissions for the good of future generations.

Acid Water

A water which is naturally acid with or without the additional effect of *acid rain* will have been formed over acid rocks (igneous) and/or soils. In Scotland the existence of peat deposits in and around lochs normally creates an acidic environment. Heavy rain causes spate conditions and the run off from peat can temporarily alter the pH of a neutral to *alkaline water*. Because of this effect, pH monitoring of lakes and streams must be done over specific intervals during the year to gain a true picture. A light run off of acidic water into an alkaline environment creates a neutral pH and is not harmful to fish, however trout and most of their invertebrate food cannot exist once the pH level falls below pH3. Trout in slightly acidic waters can still flourish and grow providing competition for food is not too intense and there is a varied food supply coming from both aquatic and terrestrial sources.

Across and Down

In UK river fishing one of the most traditional and best known ways of fishing a *wet* fly is to cast it out 'across and down'. This means putting the fly line across the current of a river and then letting it swing round naturally in the current. As most of a trout's food in streams comes down to them on the flow, it is important to keep control of the line so the fly and not the line gets presented to the fish first. See also *Mending Line*.

Action

Action is a generic UK term covering any goings-on exciting or otherwise, in and around the trouts' world. Anglers will often ask one another if they

River fishing 'across and down'.

have 'seen any action'. This normally means have they caught anything or at least had a *'rise'* or an 'offer' at their fly. The term probably has parallels with soldiers going into battle who once they have engaged an enemy are said to have 'seen action'. If the answer to the enquiry is positive then the next question will normally be about what fly was used and so the chat is initiated and extended.

Action (Rod)

The term action when applied to a rod is how the *rod* bends and flexes as it is used to cast out a fly line. Gone forever are the days when you simply picked up a fly rod and got on with it. As manufacturing techniques have advanced we are now faced with many more decisions over which rod we will require for the type of fishing we are about to undertake. Today you have rods with an apparent multiplicity of 'actions' but to keep it simple stick to three basic flexes of the fly rod. A 'through' action means the rod is soft and flexible along most of its length. Manufacturers argue that this gives a delicate presentation in tight corners or is useful where a slow roll type cast is the most commonly used. That's the plus side, the minuses are that through action rods are really hard work in strong winds and can fail on big distances. A 'middle' or 'middle to tip' action rod is probably the most popular type as this allows reasonable distance casting while still allowing a degree of feel. It only flexes as its name suggests and does not have the floppy effect of a through action. The 'tip' or 'fast' action rod is meant to give tight loops and high line speed while throwing the fly a heck of a long way, it is more difficult to control and even when it is done correctly there is no guarantee the trout are lying forty yards off!

Adams

The 'Adams' is a superb dry fly with multi-purpose uses. It is an American design first created by Ray Bergman as an all-rounder hatching insect. Nowadays its usage is worldwide which says a lot about its durability in attracting trout. Because of its subtle shades of brown, ginger and grey the Adams is a real never-fail-me pattern. Going river fishing without an Adams is the equivalent of going fishing without a reel, not something you would want to do too often. However it is just as effective on stillwaters from Spring to Autumn. The English equivalent is likely to be a *Wickham's Fancy* which has a heavier quill wing and shiny gold body but is otherwise rather similar. Both produce fine results throughout the season.

Adaptation

Having enough skill and sense to be able to adapt your fishing techniques to the *conditions* is perhaps the key element of successful fishing. Quite

13

simply what worked a day, month or a year ago might not work tomorrow because there are so many subtle changes in a trout's environment that we can have difficulty keeping up with it all. It pays to adapt and go with the flow rather than sticking to the same old thing, 'if it ain't broke don't fix it' but 'if it ain't working, change it'. Adapting might mean doing something as simple as using a dry fly on an otherwise screamingly obvious wet fly water or it might mean a whole change in fishing style. A good example of this is fishing for sea trout in salt water. In fresh water you would normally let the fly swing round in the current, in salt water you need a fast retrieve as the fish want something to chase. That in a nutshell is adapting to the conditions but you would be surprised how many of us forget or fail to make the effort to be flexible.

Aerialise

This is one of those fishy terms not really found in everyday language. If you aerialise a fly line you make a cast or two to put it in the air. Rods vary in their capacity to aerialise line quickly. A tip to middle or tip *action* rod picks line of the water in a relative flash, through action rods might need a few attempts to get there. If you need to aerialise line quickly and it involves a change of direction, try pointing the rod at the rising fish first and then lift off and cast at it. This should work unless it's a lousy wind and your line is very light.

Aerial Route

When you hook a trout on the fly it will often follow a few standard ploys to escape your attentions. Some fish will bore down as deep as they can and remain under water and out of sight as much as possible. Others will do the exact opposite and take the aerial route. Sea trout and good quality rainbows used to clear, shallow waters will normally leap and crash around like acrobats on speed whereas lake trout normally do the opposite as for them safety appears to lie beneath the waves. Research into *trout behaviour* indicates this type of aerial route is often determined genetically. In the UK, trout of the East coast are much more likely to exhibit acrobatic tendencies than West coast fish. It is something to do with East coast fish retaining roving pelagic memories and behaving more like sea trout even when landlocked.

AFTM

AFTM has been around ever since the American Federation of Tackle Manufacturers decided to come up with a table of line weights to assist anglers in choosing a fly line suited to their own rod. Light powder puff fly lines are classed around the 2 mark and heavyweight headbangers are classed up to 9 AFTM. Lines most comfortable to cast with a trout rod are probably between 5 and 7 in most situations. You will need 7/8 lines in exposed areas with high winds but can get away with a 5 on a little sheltered brook. Each rod will have an AFTM rating printed on it near the butt section and you should use the recommended weight of line. Too heavy a line will stress the rod and cause excessive wear and tear while too light a line can take a week to achieve any distance in a strong wind.

Age of Trout

As a trout grows older it does not necessarily grow bigger especially once it has reached maturity around the age of three. A trout only grows to a size that can be sustained by its immediate environment. Avoid assuming trout are babies just because they appear very small when you catch them. It is quite possible to catch a trout eight inches long and eight years old especially in nutrient-poor small streams. Conversely a trout eight inches long can be between one and two years old in a rich fertile environment. Telling the age of a trout is best done by scaling, which means reading the growth rings found in fish scales under a microscope. It's something of a specialist art but gives a good indication of growth according to its age.

Agile Darter

You might be forgiven for thinking this is a brilliant name for a trout but it is actually to do with the food the trout consumes. An agile darter is a class of *nymph* which exhibits a bit more movement than the rest which are known as burrowers, silt crawlers, laboured swimmers and stone clingers. The darter nymphs tend to be found mainly around the edges of weed beds rather than on the base of the river or lake. If truth be told it is doubtful whether trout make that much of a conscious decision on whether to take a burrower or a darter especially if they are all being cascaded down to them on a fast current. Only in slow moving pools or stillwaters do trout have more time to size up their prey. Imitations of agile darters include Pheasant Tail Nymphs tied with brown or olive coloured bodies.

Aggression

It is often said the first trout you catch out of the pond will be the most aggressive, certainly it's the most greedy. Some trout show more naturally inherent 'up front' tendencies than others and the classic example of this is the rainbow trout which is often more bold than the more cautious shy brown. Fishers use a variety of flies to stimulate this aggressive response. In the UK traditional patterns like the *Zulu*, *Soldier Palmer* and *Dunkeld* are all designed to make a trout angry enough to grab at them. Lures for rainbows provoke a similar response as do American streamers. One branch of thinking purports that brown trout which retain particular parr

A beautiful trout caught with a fly designed to stimulate an aggressive response.

marks into adulthood (see also *Parr Marked Trout*) are more aggressive than those without. Certainly when the fish are parr size they need lots of aggression to survive at all and it is considered that some retain this marking as a sexual 'look at me I'm big and fierce' signal to the ladies once they reach maturity.

Alder Fly

The Alder fly is thought to be a distant relation of some of the earliest flies tied in the UK. Certainly the *Treatise* of the fifteenth century contains a similar pattern called a Drake Fly, then it reappears in the eighteenth century *Bowlkers Art of Angling* as an Orle Fly. Charles Kingsley puts his name to it in the mid ninteenth century and is generally credited with today's design. Alders are trees found all over the UK and they harbour a mass of insects, so it seems likely the Alder Fly is simply meant as a general rather than specific representation. Whatever its origins it's a terrific and often underrated trout fly equally effective on both still and moving water. In its simplest form the Alder is tied in size 12 to 16 with a bronze peacock herl body, a black or brown hen head hackle and a speckled grouse wing. It is so versatile that it will mimic anything from an *olive* to a *sedge*, even a *mayfly*. For some reason it's not a fashionable fly but it's certainly one that has stood the test of time and often catches when others fail.

Algae

The collective term algae covers a multitude of little photosynthetic organisms found within salt and freshwater systems. Most types of algae form an essential link in the *food chain* for trout as the invertebrate life like snails and other molluscs feed off them. If there is little or no algae present the food chain falls at the first hurdle and trout can have a lean time of it. Conversely if a water becomes over enriched for example by phosphate fertiliser run off from surrounding agriculture, algae can become over abundant and choke the system. Algae blooms on water where there is little or no flushing cleansing action can be toxic to wildlife, blue green algae scum on rich *stillwaters* being the classic example of this unwanted effect. A bloom in May and June is a normal occurrence once more sunlight hits the water, and is only disruptive to fishing if it gets out of hand and causes deoxygenation of the water.

Alkaline Water

Providing a trout water is not over weighted with alkaline substances (a solution of over pH 9 becomes toxic) an alkaline habitat is more conducive to fish growth than an acid one. Waters with increased alkalinity have calcium, sodium and similar minerals dissolved in

17

solution. These minerals would normally emanate from a limestone-based (alkaline rock and/or clay) environment. Where the main source of water is from springs permeating through limestone, the water is almost certainly going to be alkaline. Alkaline water increases plant and invertebrate life and more food and shelter equals more and usually bigger trout. A simple test to see whether a water is essentially alkaline is to look for the presence of Gammarus or *freshwater shrimp*. These little creatures cannot survive in acidic water and finding them present will almost certainly guarantee an ideal trout habitat. This sampling is more reliable than using a pH meter which only shows what is happening in the water at a given time not throughout the whole year. In the UK there are pockets of limestone scattered across the country from the Caithness lochs in the far north of Scotland to the chalkstreams of Hampshire.

Ally's Shrimp

The Ally's Shrimp is essentially a universally popular salmon fly tied by Ally Gowans of Pitlochry, Scotland. You might think it has no place in a book

Ally's Shrimp.

about trout but this fly is so versatile that it is often used for sea trout and is known to hook the odd big brown or rainbow as well. The deep orange colour of this fly is its main attraction especially in fast flowing rivers. Even though it is tied on a double hook the trout don't seem to mind at all and will often seize the fly even when you are determinedly fishing for salmon. Orange almost always stimulates a smash and grab response (see *Aggression*) and trout almost certainly snatch this fly out of annoyance rather than because it looks like an insect. In the UK small fish known as *sticklebacks* develop an orange flash during their reproductive cycle and therefore big trout might see the Ally's Shrimp as a small bait fish.

Amadou
Amadou is a highly water absorbent fungus found clinging in wavy bulbous clumps to the side of trees. In the UK it is less commonly found now but can still be seen occasionally on Scottish birch trees in mature mixed woodland. Amadou was first used in dentistry in the nineteenth century to stem blood and saliva flow. During that era it made a transition into angling to dry out a sodden fly – perhaps a lateral thinking dentist went fishing and took some along with him. The great and the good like G. E. M. Skues swore by it for a time. Nowadays its been supplanted by modern chemicals including silicone sprays and wipes. Basically there is nothing more environmentally friendly to dry a fly than spongy amadou, but times change and its less popular now.

Anchor Ice
In streams where the winter air temperature regularly falls below minus 20 degrees C a strange phenomenon occurs. Instead of ice forming on the water surface, the subsurface sediment starts to freeze and clouds of suspended tiny ice crystals known as frazil ice drift downstream. These clouds then attach themselves to gravel, rocks, tree roots and any other structures on the bottom and form Anchor ice. Any rise in temperature from the sun rays causes the Anchor ice to detach itself and a horrible mixture of ice rock and gravel is uprooted and propelled downstream. It is thought that this uprooting of gravel can take with it a fair number of trout eggs thus causing a higher than normal winter mortality.

Anglers' Curse
In the UK those clouds of small white/pale flies known as caenis are also known as the Anglers' Curse. Once a profuse caenis hatch comes on the water trout fishing becomes almost impossible as trout simply fixate on these tiny beasts and ignore most of your offerings. Though there are some willing to imitate them your best hope is usually a large pale fly fished amongst the millions of little ones, either that or go home!

Angling

It goes without question that we all enjoy angling but oddly enough the term is derived from an Old English word meaning a fish hook with a bend or 'angle' in it. Through time, angling became a term associated with using a rod, as the fifteenth century *Treatise* puts it 'Fysshynge wyth an angle'. 'Angling' therefore came to mean using only a rod, line and hook rather than the much wider term of 'Fishing'. Going fishing in Great Britain in the old days covered a range of methods principally using nets in a variety of ways including 'cobbling' and 'dragging'. Cobbling was more associated with stringing a net over a river while dragging meant dragging a net through a loch or lake. Both methods were pretty indiscriminate taking out all and any fish usually for the purpose of food. Leistering was also part of fishing and this involved throwing a sharp forked metal-tipped stick shaped like a trident (spear) at an unsuspecting fish usually a salmon. Equally ferocious methods included burning the water which involved setting light to oil on the water surface thereby suffocating fish and even dynamiting was used, all this in the name of fishing! 'Anglers' got their name simply from using the kinder method of rod, hook and line.

Apache Trout

The Apache trout is indigenous to the wilder parts of Arizona and New

Arizona – Apache trout country.

Mexico regions of the US. At one time this trout was under threat of extinction from a combination of factors including *habitat* degradation, *competition* from other fish such as the rainbow trout and climate change. However thanks to the efforts of the Apache Indians and other like minded fishers, pure populations of this beautiful golden olive trout are still to be found notably in the streams of the Fort Apache Indian Reservation and the White Mountains of Arizona. The trout occupy the headwaters of the Little Colorado, Salt and San Francisco Rivers and have also been stocked into nearby small lakes. 'Apaches' are top quality trout beautifully speckled with shining burnished gold flanks, orange fins and have a heavy spotting on the tail. They have comparable markings and colouration to the similarly stunning Gila Trout of the Gila River of Arizona and New Mexico and are a trout to be conserved and cherished.

Arbor
The drum of a fishing *reel* which holds the fly line is also referred to as an arbor. Though you would think there is not much fashion and style

Trout captured using a large arbor reel.

revolving around a piece of cold machinery like a fly-fishing reel, the hip thing now is to use large arbor reels particularly in stillwater fishing. These are considered very useful as they can store more line and backing and the wider drum allows for a faster stripping off and rewinding of the fly line. Traditional reels with a smaller drum have a tendency to corkscrew poorer quality fly lines and encourage awkward and tight circles in the line which can take an age to straighten out (see also *Memory*). At the moment large arbor reels win the day especially in lake angling in the UK but then there is always a question mark over where fashion will lead us next.

Arctic Charr
Arctic charr are found in the northern hemisphere with good populations existing in Britain, Scandinavia and northern parts of Canada. While their torpedo shape is similar to brown trout, their markings are very different with pale red, yellow or orange spots on a blue/green background. Fins are orange with a white tip and when caught the fish often resemble beautiful little goldfish. In the UK and Scandinavia, Arctic charr are mainly found in deep lakes and lochs while in the North West Territories of Canada river populations of this char are relatively common. While it is true these fish mainly feed deep on plankton they can adapt to conditions and are known to consume molluscs, crustaceans, larvae and even other fish. In the UK studies have been done on char in Loch Rannoch, Scotland. This research showed two separate types of char known as Pelagic (upper water plankton feeder) and Benthic (lower water bottom feeder) coexisting in the loch yet consuming differing food items. Because of their generally deeper lying habitat, few anglers in the UK fish specifically for charr but the fish form an essential part of the diet of the *Ferox* so it has its work cut out with natural predators anyway.

Artificial
If you are casting with an 'artificial' it is a fly which looks like an artificial representation of the real insect. The origin of this term is obscure for though the actual word meaning a copy of the real thing has been around for years, it appears to be only comparatively recently introduced into angling terminology probably during the nineteenth century. To use an artificial usually means to use a fly which is not a general *attractor pattern*. For example a Great Red Sedge looks like the real insect and can be classed immediately as an artificial while a Blue Zulu looks like nothing remotely to do with the insect world and was originally designed purely to stimulate an aggressive response, still technically an 'artificial' but poles apart from the close representation! It all gets a bit like splitting hairs rather than splitting wings but there we are...

Attractor Patterns

Attractors are UK fly patterns which bear little or no relation to any particular item of food a trout would consume. The term arose to differentiate between vaguely dressed flies and exact imitations of the real thing. Attractors are normally fished on a fast *retrieve* and elicit a smash and grab response, see *Artificial*.

Back End Fishing

If you fish at the back end of the season its simply fishing in late Autumn or the 'Fall'. This is principally a term used by UK salmon anglers but trout anglers also use it occasionally. Back end fishing for trout can be highly productive if the conditions are benign. In both rivers and stillwaters larger trout start to become more active and they will begin to travel toward their spawning beds grabbing opportunistic feeding as they progress. In doing so the fish become more vulnerable and the crafty angler knows this and intercepts them. Should the trout be female and already showing signs of *egg* development it is better for future generations of fish to return her and let her continue on her way.

Backing

Fisher folk will sometimes use the phrase 'stripped down to the backing' and although the non fisher's mind might boggle a bit at this, it is actually an innocent description of a heavy fish taking all the fly line off the reel drum in a fast run for freedom, so much so that the backing appears. Backing is therefore useful for two things: one to extend the length of a fly line and two to act as a cushion and filler for the reel to stop the line corkscrewing in too tight circles. It is made of a strong thin braided cord and lasts an age unless stored on the reel in a very soggy wet state in which case it can be prone to mould. If you fish specimen trout waters a lot ensure you have a really good joining knot between backing and fly line otherwise you are liable to part company at the vital moment.

Backing up

The technique of backing up a pool on a river involves casting your line across and then taking a couple of steps upstream. While most *dry fly* fishing is executed by casting directly upstream, 'backing up' involves casting a *wet fly* across and down and then moving upstream. The idea behind it is to reposition yourself above the wet fly in order to allow a better presentation of the fly as it swings round in a slow moving *current*. In slack water casting a wet fly by the traditional means of 'across and *down'* can sometimes lead to an unnatural belly in the line, backing up solves this nuisance. Although it's a salmon orientated tactic it is also pretty useful for brown trout in deep, slow-moving pools.

Bag Limit

If a bag limit has been imposed on a fishery by *management* it means you will be allowed to catch and keep up to, say, three fish and then anything else caught must be returned. In the UK bag limits are mainly imposed on busy stocked fisheries, wild fisheries impose self restraint or ask for *catch and release* at certain times of the year. Bag limits are a conservation action of sorts but obtusely they can place something of a burden on fishers to make their limit especially on heavily stocked waters where it is looked upon as failure if you do not catch your quota. In some quarters this is known as 'limititus' a silly but nevertheless apt term for those determined not to go home without a prescribed number of fish!

Baggot

In the UK a baggot is a mature female sea trout which has run up from the sea into freshwater but has not spawned. When caught she will show signs of retained *eggs* which she has not been able to shed. Baggots usually become egg bound when for one reason or another they have been deprived of normal access to spawning redds or have not been able to attract a mate. In practice it is quite unusual to capture a baggot, and more commonly caught in early season are out of condition sea trout (see *Kelts*) which have managed to spawn but have not yet recovered to full condition.

Balance

Good technique in casting a fly line comes from being able to balance your body during lifting off and propelling the line forward on to the water. You will know immediately if your body is not balanced as the forward cast will land awkwardly. To assist in balancing your body and maintaining poise during casting keep your back straight and use your *free hand* (the hand holding the fly line as opposed to the rod) as a sort of counter weight. In other words the free arm elbow should be hinged and relaxed and should not cross over the body or be held straight and rigid at your side. *Casting* a fly is not a difficult operation – it just seems that way when your balance is off.

Bank Fishing

Except for the widest rivers which might need a boat, bank fishing is the accepted norm in river fishing either progressing upstream with a dry fly or downstream with a wet. Sometimes *wading* is involved, sometimes it is

Misako Ishimura shows good 'balance' and poise.

just launching your fly from the bank to where you think the trout are lying. Stillwater angling is a different bag however as you often have the choice of whether to fish from a boat or go on the bank. Advantages of bank fishing on stillwaters include being able to go back and cover a rising trout again and from a different angle. In a *drifting boat* you will only be able to cast to a rising fish maybe twice before you are propelled past him on the wind. Disadvantages of stillwater bank fishing include lengthy walks if the hot spots are a distance from your starting point or if the wind changes suddenly and leaves you on the wrong bank. Boats are much quicker at putting you from one end to the other in a short space of time. Bear in mind that whether bank fishing a river or a lake you should aim to travel along the bank and cover new trout territories, standing still will only capture what is in front of you if anything.

Barbless Hooks

Using fly hooks with the barb flattened is a common practice in the US however in the UK the practice is less popular. Detractors claim the hook hold in a trout's jaw is more secure with a barb and that barbless hooks can cause suffering for trout as they squirm around on the hook. Apparently it becomes more deeply embedded without a stopping barb. On the plus side the releasing of a trout is generally quicker with a barbless hook. If you reach down the leader and give the hook a twist and/or shake the trout will normally come off thus saving on the stressful time the fish is out of the water. Barbless hooks are commonly used in *catch and release* fishing.

Barometric Pressure

It is thought that trout are sensitive to barometric pressure and come on and go off the feed according to the rise and fall of the barometer. A rising glass usually heralds more settled weather (high pressure) and is thought to be more productive than falling (low) pressure. The theory has never been proven completely accurate as there are many other variables involved in successful fishing including length of experience and general tactical skills. However it does seem to be the case that a deep 'low' will put trout down for a variable space of time – they are after all much more sensitive to these things than us lesser mortals.

Basket

'A good basket of fish' is an old British term still occasionally used meaning a good catch. It is principally associated with the wicker *creel* used to transport fish from the water to the table. In the 1600s baskets known in Old English as 'bafkets' were sometimes suspended in rivers being left agape to trap fish (normally salmon) as they tried to ascend the stream. This was a simple method akin to using a net, and in the end commercially-made nets were to prove much more efficient. In the 1700s a measure of the catch was a 'barrel' with UK rivers yielding so many barrels of salmon per annum. Barrels and baskets therefore have similar historic meanings.

Bass

While bass covers a wide range of fish species from American freshwater 'small mouth bass' to British salt water 'sea bass', a bass can also mean the bag used to keep trout fresh. Originally a trout bass was made out of woven materials, straw being replaced by canvas. Though they keep the trout fresher than a plastic bag they can be very smelly objects especially if not washed out for a while. In fact it might well be said a stinky bass in a hot car greatly furthers the cause for *catch and release*.

Beaching Trout

If you wish to keep your captured trout rather than return it, and you have no *landing net* then you have little option but to try and beach it. This simply means running the trout head first up and aground on the bank. This sounds a simple enough task but if the trout is spirited, it is during the beaching that things can and will go askew. If you try and beach a trout before it is *played out* i.e. ready to surrender after the battle royal, the probability of it flipping itself free of the hook is high. Bear in mind that beaching fish can remove some of the protective mucous covering their scales and therefore you should only attempt this manoeuvre if you are definitely wanting your catch for the table.

Beads

Gone are the days when the heads and/or bodies of flies were made from little more than floss, fur or feather. Today we have fishermen making their favourite patterns out of what look like dolls' beads. It is unclear who first thought of this novel deployment but the use of beads has caught on in a big way. They are made with a range of materials from heavy tungsten to lightweight shiny plastic and are used to represent either the eyes, head or by stringing them along the hook you can make the whole body of a nymph or small fish. Perhaps not for the *purist*, however they undoubtedly provide a new trout attracting dimension to your fishing.

Beat

Scotland is the home of salmon and trout fishing and if you were to fish one of the pristine rivers you would do so on a 'beat'. It is not clear where the term beat came from but it is likely to be military as in walking or marching to the beat of a drum. A beat is therefore a designated stretch of river, usually numbered, and once booked and paid for you are allowed to travel

27

its length but no further in pursuit of fish. Some beats will have specific rules governing this progress, for example you may have to fish entirely downstream, finish and then walk back up to the top to start again. Beat descriptions will mainly refer to salmon pools as this fish always has priority recognition in Scotland, however be assured that trout also lie amongst the King of Fish but in the past, brownies were foolishly treated as a lesser game species.

Beetles

Trout eat an extraordinary array of food and beetles form a rather underrated but nevertheless important part of this catholic diet. In the UK the most important beetles are probably the Coch Y Bonddu or Bracken Clock and the Whirligig beetle. The former has a greenish head and brown/red wings and is quite small. On a warm June day they are often blown off the shore into the mouths of waiting trout who accept them with gusto. The Welsh fly, Coch Y Bonddu is an admirable imitation which has stood the test of time. The Whirligig beetle is purely aquatic and is most prominent in the weedy shallows of stillwaters in the summer months where they quite literally whirl around in tiny circles attracting trout to come in and take a bite. Black and Peacock Spiders do for these little guys. Rather similar is the Lesser Water Boatman or Corixa which is most prevalent during late summer. This little insect swims up and down from the beds of lakes and slow moving rivers in order to take in more oxygen which it cleverly keeps as a bubble of air on its belly. The Coch Y Bonddu *artificial* admirably doubles as a Corixa.

Behaviour (in Trout)

Trout behaviour is a fascinating science. If you know why trout are behaving in a particular way, it should improve your chances of catching them. Fish behaviour is based on instinctive rather than intellectual responses. Instincts drive a trout to feed, to find shelter from predators and to spawn to further the species. In wild fish populations these activities will follow a genetic imprint going back many generations. *Genes* will determine where and when the trout spawn, whether the fish are predominantly free rising or bottom hugging, how aggressive or shy they are, what size they grow to and so on. Different strains of trout exhibit differing characteristics. In the UK the *Leven trout* more resembles a torpedo-shaped silver sea trout used to feeding freely on insects and crustaceans in shallow water while the *Ferox* is a chunky darker gold trout given to feeding off other smaller fish and dwelling at a depth of forty feet or more. In the USA there are well defined differences between the aggressive *rainbows* and the more secretive cautious *brown* trout. Over time restocking of waters has put paid to some specific trout traits with intermingling of genes creating hybrid behaviour. True trout behaviour is best seen where pure native indigenous stocks still exist.

Bibio

The Bibio is a wonderfully versatile Irish lake/lough pattern. It was originally tied by a Major Roberts in the early 1960s as a sea trout fly made to represent the natural heather fly Bibio Pomonae which is rather like a small bee with black body, flat wings and red legs. However the artificial representation Bibio is now in universal use on UK stillwaters for all types of trout. The pattern's success is due to two things. One, its simple colours of black and red with silver rib are undoubtedly the most useful colour combinations in brown and sea trout angling, and two, its black *palmered* hackle has wonderful light and air trapping qualities which give the fly a realistic pulsing movement in the water. The best dressings of a Bibio are of a sparse delicate tying, anything too heavy on the body or hackle creates a solid ball of wool and fluff which hits the water like a small bomb. Aim for a *Spider* look as this makes the fly more attractive and less scary to trout. Oddly enough there does not seem to be an American equivalent to this fly perhaps as palmered flies are a peculiarly British trait.

Biot

A biot is a predominantly American term for a hackle feather used in fly construction. Goose and turkey biots are often used for making all or part of the body of the fly for example John Gierach cites the 'Frying Pan Biot Green Drake' and the 'Biot Pale Morning Dun' in his book of *Good Flies*. The term 'biots' is now more common amongst the newer (younger?) generation of fly tyers in the UK, some of the older generation still refer to hackles as hackles and have done with it!

Bi-visible Flies

This term is relatively common on both sides of the Atlantic and simply means that a dry fly has been made extra visible with the addition of a lighter coloured hackle in front of the normal head hackle. Providing it is not overdone the combination of light and dark hackles can give a more natural appearance. Natural insects are not a solid black or solid brown and their wings have a filmy appearance with a soft mix of colour. The same idea can be applied to *dubbing* by mixing in different colours for a more subtle appearance.

Black Flies

In the UK one of the most killing colours for trout flies is black or at least a dark shade. In the *Treatise* there is a fly mentioned for May called the Black Louper which is similar to the Black Palmer, one of our most ancient flies with origins as far back as the fourteenth century. It is little more than twists of black hackle over a black body yet it has stood the test of time admirably. If you think about it the more a fly sinks down in the water the more its colour becomes monochrome and eventually completely black. Little wonder therefore the first flies tied were usually dark dull affairs. Black Palmers are particularly useful in Scottish loch fishing where a team of flies is used. The Black Palmer is often used on the top *dropper* as it creates a little wake on the water surface and acts as an attractor to trout.

Black Fly

In marsh lands for example in Alaska and Scandinavia there is a particularly nasty biting insect known as black fly and which is equivalent or possibly even worse than the Scottish midge. Strong insect repellent and a head net are a must when these voracious insects are about. Main hatching months for these little beasts are July and August so beware.

Black Gnat

Black Gnats are particularly profuse in the Spring when clouds of those whiskery dark insects hatch from the land and then flutter in columns in the margins of stillwater and in the slower sections of a stream during calm weather. In the 1600s that illustrious English angler Charles Cotton wrote about using an imitation of the Black Gnat presumably as a general copy of a small *terrestrial* black midge. Anglers now use Black Gnats to represent a variety of small dark insects, anything from a reed smut to a *Bibio*. There are numerous variations of Gnats but one of the most productive is listed in E M Tod's book *Wet Fly Fishing*. It has a black silk body, small black hen hackle at head tied sparse and a pale starling wing and should be tied on 14 to 16 hooks. Some versions use a peacock herl body which can end up rather squat in shape, Tod's Black Gnat avoids this bulk.

Black Trout

In water which is very dark in colour, for example a Scottish loch with a very high peat content, the brown trout assume an almost black coat instead of the more usual golden brown. While this phenomenon highlights the ability of trout to camouflage themselves in their immediate environment, the black trout tend to be in rather poor condition. Their lack of spirit is usually put down to their struggle to thrive in what is essentially *acid water*. Any acidic environment with a lack of good feeding puts added *stress* on the trout and can cause the trout to develop a darker skin and extra coat of mucous in order to survive.

Blae

The word blae is principally associated with flies like the Blae and Black. Blae is an old Scots word of Nordic origin. It means grey or bluish grey, blaeberries are a particularly sweet ground berry fruit found in some Scottish moors in summer. These small berries have a characteristic blue grey hue. The Blae and Black is a mighty useful if rather nondescript fly good for any hatch of black midge especially early to mid season. In Ireland these black midge hatches are known as *Duck fly*. The fly can be made in any size from 10 to 16 and it has a black body, silver rib, head hackle of black hen and medium starling wing. Tom Stewart, in his book *Two Hundred Popular Flies*, recommends a red feather tail as a neat addition but both tyings work well.

Blank

In trout fishing there are two connotations to blank. The first means not catching a single trout during a day's outing and the second refers to the parts of a rod. If you buy rod blanks it means the rod is in basic wand form without any rings, bindings, reel seats etc. Today rod blanks are mainly made of carbon fibre material.

Bloodworm

Silt-dwelling bloodworms are midge larvae and they form a useful supplement to the trout's diet especially if there is little to tempt fish on or near the surface. Bloodworms are instantly recognisable as the small tube-like red worm found during an autopsy of stomach contents. Some trout fixate on these and achieve good weights despite the smallness of this food. Famous Scottish angler of old, P D Malloch circa 1909, remarked on the obsession of Loch *Leven* trout in taking these tiny morsels in his historic book *Life History and Habits of the Salmon*. Traditional flies with splashes of red like the *Zulu* or the Peter Ross have been used for aeons before the more exact imitations of bloodworm (sometimes made with *beads*) came along in the 1980s. The theory behind using robust general attractor patterns rather than exact replicas is more to do with interrupting the trout's feeding patterns and stimulating an aggressive response.

Boat Fishing

Boats can be an advantage in any type of stillwater fishing. They get you where you want to go quickly instead of tramping for miles along the shore and give you a head start in reaching those parts just out of *bank* casting range. Boats are also great for those who want to fish sitting down and providing you have all the many accoutrements required with you, the day afloat should be a pleasant one. There are however disadvantages

Boat fishing.

and these are mainly associated with the weather. High winds and boats are very hard work if not dangerous, engines can break down or refuse to start, *drogues* can refuse to operate or entangle the fish of a lifetime, rollocks might suddenly part company and so on. Poorly maintained boats are an absolute menace suddenly springing leaks and requiring manic bailing to reach the shore again. *Buoyancy aids* are an absolute must for boat fishing and must be worn despite heat and bulk, tragedies occur too often. Fishing from the boat has to be done on a *drift*, i.e. with the wind more or less behind. Flies are cast out *loch style* and worked back towards the boat, exciting fishing if the elements don't get the better of you.

Bobber

Fishing with a bobber is an American term for fishing with a float or at least a *sight indicator*. Bobbers can be made of round brightly coloured polystyrene balls or simply be a large bright piece of feather/wool. This is attached on to the leader at a prescribed distance above the fly depending on what depth you want the *artificial* to be fishing. A bobber is often used when nymph fishing to give some indication when the fly has been taken sub surface. Once the bobber twitches the fisher should strike and hopefully the trout will stay on.

Bob Fly

Most forms of *loch style* angling involve using teams of wet flies attached by *droppers* on a long leader. The bob fly is the top dropper of the team. These flies are cast out and worked back towards the angler predominantly when loch or lake fishing though historically teams of flies have also been used in UK river angling to great effect. In Scotland W C Stewart circa 1850s relates that anglers used up to twelve flies on their 'cast' or leader and that this was a common method for both still and flowing water. In the early 1800s *dry fly* was not yet invented and the bob fly positioned at the top end of the cast was therefore used as an attractor or wake fly. When the team of flies is retrieved the bob fly makes its appearance first causing a disturbance on the water surface and possibly acting as a magnet to the trout. Fish might lunge at the bob fly or once drawn near, may have a go at one of the other patterns trailing behind.

Boil

A boil is a particularly exciting action made when a trout is vigorously feeding. The water surface suddenly seems to part and bulge as the trout has come up and turned full on into an attractive food item just below or emerging on the surface. A few tell tale bubbles are often left after the fish has risen. Anglers should try and get their fly near that boil as quickly as possible for the fish is definitely in taking mood. The bigger the boil the bigger the trout as the whole body of the fish is involved in this movement.

Bolognese Rods

Long pole-like rods used principally for bait fishing in the Mediterranean region are called Bolognese rods. They are light, hollow rods up to twenty feet or so in length. There is no casting action as such with these rods, a slight flick to propel the float and attached bait out is all that is required. Bolognese rods are worthy of a mention however as they bear close resemblance to some of the earliest rods used in trout fishing. *Dapping* rods are almost identical and these rods are used in similar fashion being simply held upright and letting the wind blow out a light floss line with dapping fly attached. It is likely that dapping equipment was the first type of *rod* used in the UK prior to the invention of the *reel*. Bolognese rods may therefore be distant relatives of the first British rods ever used.

Brackish water

Areas where fresh water meets and mingles with salt water are known in

Bolognese rods in use in Maltese waters.

the UK as brackish. Where there are strong incoming tides, brackish water may occur several miles inland as the seawater is pushed upstream by the force of the tide. If you are unsure whether brackish water exists where you are fishing dip a finger in and test for salt. In Scotland fishing in brackish (tidal) waters is usually 'free' though in the future the law may be changed governing this activity.

Braided Leaders

If you wish you can extend the length of your fly line and possibly achieve a better turn over by then using a braided leader might help. This device joins the leader to the line by means of a length of braided flexible cord. These are treated to make them float or sink to various depths. The original idea was probably to alleviate the need for a vast array of different fly lines. By putting on a braided leader the angler could change the depth at which he/she was fishing at a stroke. Initial problems of joining and changing the braided leader quickly have now been ironed out with clever little loop attachments. Some anglers swear by these but if you are a traditionalist using teams of flies on droppers this device may not offer as much flexibility. See also *Tapered Leaders*.

Braided Loops

For many years the only way to join nylon to fly line was by a knot. This highly useful piece of kit does away with those knotty problems as once in place a braided loop acts as a permanent connector. A short hollow braided sleeve with a loop at one end is fed over the end of the fly line, a thicker plastic sleeve is slid down over this, a dab of glue applied to keep all in place and hey presto a little braided loop now allows you to tie on your leader without fuss. Not all modern inventions are that clever but this is one of them.

Breaking Strain – BS

It might be thought that this term should refer to the frustrated angler who after a flurry of mad casting fails to connect with anything and goes home in a fit of pique having reached his breaking strain. However it actually (more boringly) refers to the maximum pressure that can be applied to your *leader* before it is liable to snap. Thus 4lb BS means a trout has to thump this with an almighty 4lb plus of pressure before the leader might (or might not) break. Such is the quality of leader material these days that any breaks occur mainly at the joining knots rather than in the material itself. Hence it is important to change the leader if you find wind knots. It is quite possible to play and land a 6lb trout on unsullied 4lb nylon providing it is done with skill and care.

Breeding Trout

The science of breeding fish is an ancient one. The Chinese were known to be expert fish breeders, fish culture was popular during the Roman Empire, and monks of the fourteenth century also artificially bred fish in ponds. In Europe serious breeding of trout was first recorded in the eighteenth century in France and Germany and the practice became increasingly widespread through the nineteenth century. The French invented an ingenious method of fish propagation which involved a system of glass rods or grilles. Trout eggs were laid out on these grilles and allowed to incubate instead of being placed on gravel beds which were more liable to silt up and suffocate the eggs. This glass rod system was very successful and led to a boom in trout restocking for sporting purposes. In Britain the Victorians in the late 1800s stocked numerous freshwaters avidly and this practice was to continue apace until the First World War. Today in the UK, the emphasis has swung from brown trout and salmon hatchery farms privately run on large sporting estates (common in the Victorian era) to commercial enterprises centred principally on rainbow trout rather than browns. While modern breeding methods have moved on from the days of glass rods, the prerequisite for successful culture of trout remains the same – shaded, cool, clean, well oxygenated water with a sustained flow and even temperature. Without this any fish rearing enterprise will fail.

Brook Trout

The Brook trout hails originally from North East Canada and the American East coast though its distribution is now widespread across many US States and it has also been imported into the UK. Brookies are really a type of Charr and they have wonderful colours and markings. With reddish bellies, orange fins with a white fringe, marbled vermiculations (worm-like markings) on the back and the dorsal fin and abundant red spots with a blue halo, these have got to be some of the prettiest trout around. They differ however from the *Arctic Charr* in terms of habitat and feeding. While Brook trout can survive well in shallow, muddy or peaty lakes and can also thrive in river habitats, Arctic Charr are found mainly in clean, deep water lakes. Brook trout are opportunistic feeders taking any abundant 'hatch' from snails to surface insects to other small fish while Arctic Charr feed mainly on zoo plankton and bottom dwelling larvae. Because Brookies are able to tolerate muddy habitats they are often stocked into systems which do not sustain particularly good populations of browns or rainbows. Interbreeding of Brook trout with *Brown trout* creates a Zebra or Tiger trout similar in markings to the *Marbled trout*.

Brown Trout (Brownies) from the same stillwater but showing different colouration and markings.

Brown Trout (Brownies)

Brown trout as *Salmo trutta* were originally native only to Europe and North Asia however their distribution as a much loved sporting fish is now world wide in both rivers and lakes. Fertile trout eggs were exported from Britain during the latter half of the nineteenth century to such far away places as America, New Zealand, South Africa, Australia, India and Argentina. Most of these introductions now thrive and form completely naturalised populations. The almost infinite variation of beautiful colours and markings within this one fish species is truly remarkable. Brownies' bodies can range from a silvery green hue to a deep burnished gold. Black and/or red spots dot their backs in different patterns, the tail has little or no spots and many fish have a golden flank with creamy underbelly. They are adaptable creatures and will only grow to a size which their immediate environment can sustain. Thus trout in a rich fertile water can attain significant weight providing competition is not too great while trout in an *acidic water* might only weigh a few ounces at maturity. Browns have a slightly more reclusive shy character than their American cousins the *Rainbow*, however given clean water, adequate food and shelter and a place to reproduce they will prosper in most situations. Brownies are opportunist feeders taking most food items from the bottom, mid and surface layer of water. Their diet consists of molluscs, crustaceans, insects, small fish, worms, crayfish, beetles, frogs and just about anything else that moves and they can get their jaws around. The *Sea trout* is simply a brown which has gone to sea to feed and grow and then has returned to its natal stream to spawn.

Bugs

In European countries the term, 'using bugs', is sometimes applied to the use of *Czech nymphs*. These are heavyweight nymphs designed to plummet the depths in lake fishing and trundle along the bottom of a stream. The application of weighty metals like copper or tungsten makes for a quick sinking nymph particularly useful in fast currents which would otherwise sweep away a lighter nymph. The art of how to fish these bugs is further discussed under *Czech nymphs*.

Bull Trout

The Bull trout is a charr native to NW America however during the late nineteenth century, sea trout of the British Isles were also occasionally known as Bull trout. The latter classification was largely used through Victorian times when just about any slightly different colour of trout was given a distinct name. The Bull trout of America has characteristic charr markings with light spots on a darker background however it has slightly less spectacular colours than the Brook trout. Bull trout require cool, well oxygenated habitats but do equally well in both flowing and still water. They are mainly large bottom feeders when small but then once they gain a bit of weight they will become piscivorous and predate on other small fish. Introductions of other sporting species such as rainbow or Brookies have had a deleterious effect on some Bull trout populations as they cannot cope with much competition in their habitat.

Bumbles

While you might think this term refers aptly to some anglers' vain attempts to catch trout it is actually a genus of fly first brought to light and improved upon by one of the masters of Irish trout fishing, T C Kingsmill Moore. The first Bumbles were tied during the seventeenth century in England as basic *palmered* flies however Moore set about bettering these and turning them into top class lake patterns particularly effective as bushy *dropper* patterns. Though Moore in his famous book *A Man May Fish* lists seven Bumbles he states the colour combinations are almost endless. In the UK the three best known of his Bumble series are the Golden Olive Bumble, the Claret Bumble and the Bruiser which has a

Buoyancy aids are lifesavers.

blue body and blue/black hackle. The whiskery palmer of this fly is probably the reason it attracts so many trout, it seems at times to pulse and dance through the waves. Bumbles are hard to beat on any lake in the world on a good blowy day.

Buoyancy Aids

Falling into deep and/or fast, icy cold water is a serious and sometimes life threatening business even if you consider yourself an Olympic swimmer. Wearing a buoyancy aid does two vital things: one it keeps your head above the water and two allows you to float long enough to be rescued if the hypothermia doesn't get you first. If this sounds gloomy it is meant to be, too many avoidable tragedies still occur because people don't wear a buoyancy aid. You can purchase these in a variety of forms from a highly buoyant barrel-like vest which you pull on over your head to a fishing vest with permanent float panels built in. Some fishing vests incorporate a toggle which you must pull on falling into the water. This fires a shot of gas into a *life jacket* which then fills up and keeps you above water. Other jackets automatically inflate on becoming soaking wet though these can sometimes inflate of their own accord even if you do not require them at the time. One of the neatest is two slimline bars which you wear over your fishing jacket and inflate by emergency toggle. These still allow you to cast reasonably well while some find the panel jackets a bit constricting. Whatever you choose, wear one, it could save your life.

Butcher

The Butcher is a really neat UK fly invented in 1838 by Mr Moon an English butcher by trade. It was apparently called Moon's Fly until someone changed it to its more apt name. Since then there have been several variants made of the original but the simple winged version still attracts numerous trout each season. Butchers are particularly effective at imitating small darting fish and are most effective when used as a *lure* pattern. The original dressing of red feather tail, flat silver body, black hen head hackle and mallard wing is as good as any. Fish the Butcher by letting it sink a bit before retrieving back in short jerks. The Bloody, Kingfisher and Gold Butcher are top variants of this *traditional* pattern.

Butt

Nothing rude here, the butt of the rod is simply the stub of the cork handle. There is some confusion about the term 'giving the fish butt'. While it is often interpreted as the application of brute force to bring a trout under control the term originates from ancient angling methods. When all that stood between you and the fish was a skinny strand of horse hair the easiest way to gain control was to throw the rod back over the shoulder and point or show the butt at the fish. This made maximum use of the pliability of the rod, without showing the butt the trout often got off by breaking the fine *gut*.

Buzzers

Buzzers are a peculiarly English term for artificial representations of midges (*chironomids*). These flies are sparsely tied and usually fished below the water surface. Classic examples of Buzzer tyings include the Shipmans Buzzer, Black Buzzer and Buff Buzzer. In Ireland *Duck fly* imitations are meant to imitate the early season black midge hatch and these are effectively used as buzzers. Originally the term described the hatched midge which does indeed buzz above the water, however anglers have adapted and extended the generic class to also cover midge pupae stuck in the surface film and nymphs and larvae below the surface. It is likely that *Spider* patterns of the 1800s were the forerunner of modern Buzzer patterns which only came to the fore during the rise in popularity of rainbow reservoir trout fishing in the 1970s. Some anglers will refer to fishing teams of 'Buzzer nymphs' on a slow retrieve just below the water surface. It is really all the same thing, a midge imitation of sorts.

Caddis

Caddis are the universally recognised larvae of the *Sedge fly* so beloved of anglers on both sides of the Atlantic. For a bottom dwelling grub, caddis score quite highly in the self protection stakes. Whilst in the grub stage they gather up a protective casing around their bodies. This can be made of sand, tiny stones, even twigs and the caddis entombs itself in this shell in the hope of evading predators like trout. Using its powerful front feelers to drag itself along, the caddis will crawl around tortoise-like on the bottom, munching on smaller bugs as it goes. Trout don't pay much attention to the caddis armour however and simply eat the whole grub shell and all, expelling the little stones through their gut. Slightly confusingly, some fishers refer to caddis flies when they actually mean the hatched *sedge* rather than the larvae. This creates perplexity in fly imitations. Take for example the 'Kings River Caddis' shown in Jack Dennis's wonderful book *Western Trout Fly Tying Manual*. This fly looks all the world like the dry Large Red Sedge commonly made in the UK. In Britain the larva are called caddis and can be imitated with any strong nymph pattern such as the *Hare's Ear* while the hatched sedges are imitated with various noted dry *Sedge* patterns.

Cane Rods

While there is evidence of cane rods being in use for fishing in the Far East as far back as the Chou Dynasty (221BC) the widespread use of cane in the UK only took off in the seventeenth century. At that time it was used as a whole piece (whole cane) sometimes combined with a different wood top. It is often assumed cane rods were the only forerunner to fibre glass and carbon fibre rods however woods like hazel, hickory and greenheart were also used. In the early nineteenth century British rod makers began experimenting with 'split cane' gluing together strips of cane to form a six-sided wand. These were undoubtedly the most sought after prior to modern rod developments. Some anglers still use cane particularly on rivers however its general heaviness has meant that carbon fibre rods now top the league.

Cannibal Trout

As trout are opportunistic feeders taking any morsel of protein coming their way, their ability to consume their own kind and/or other smaller fish species is inherent. However some trout show more of an inclination to become cannibalistic than others. Often this is down to the trout's size specifically what it can get its jaws around, but the *abundance factor* also comes into play. If there is a consistent profusion of small fish in the trout's vicinity then that will become a major source of food and the trout will fixate on it. If smaller brethren are scarce however then the trout must look for a more diverse diet. In the UK some old fishing books refer to *Ferox* as 'cannibal trout' resembling large toothy out of condition pike. This is an unfair description of a beautiful trout, the scrawny specimens gracing the walls of old Scottish highland fishing hotels are actually very old fish way past their best and had they not been caught and stuffed would have met their Maker very shortly.

Capes

Fly tyers buying feathers in bulk may wish to purchase a whole cape which will have been cut from the bird with all feathers still attached to the preserved skin base. This way the fly tyer has a good choice from the different length and varying thickness of hackles on the cape. Metz capes are a famous variety but nowadays there is a big selection available including capes dyed specific colours as much as the natural.

Cast

In the UK the term cast was at one time much used to describe the *leader* principally during the early to mid 1900s when *gut* or *horsehair* leaders had been replaced by more modern substitutes. Angling books of that period often refer to flies to be used on a typical 'cast' for a specific water. For example 'A cast made up of a nymph fished wet on the tail and a dry fly dropper is sometimes a good combination,' Maunsell *The Fisherman's Vade Mecum* circa 1933. Nowadays the term has more or less fallen into disuse as anglers now mainly talk in terms of *leaders* and *tippets*. The action required to propel a fly on to the water as a 'cast' is dealt with in *Casting a Fly* below.

Casting a Fly

Way back in the days when fly *lines* were nothing but a tapered twist of *horsehair* attached at the end of a rod, most attempts at casting of a fly would be dependant on wind assistance. The redoubtable British Colonel Venables circa 1662 makes mention of the physical act of casting but it appears this was more to do with dangling fly and line over the water (presumably aided by a breeze) so that the fly hit the water first and not the trailing line. It was only with the advent of *reels* (circa seventeenth and eighteenth century) and more importantly fly line materials like silk which could be stored on the reel and then pulled out to an appropriate length, that casting technique started to evolve. The *overhead* and *roll cast* as we know them today were slowly developed over time from the late seventeenth century. No credit goes to one

Casting a fly.

particular inventor over all others as casting technique seems to follow a gradual evolution keeping roughly in time with tackle developments. Today probably the best way to learn to cast is to have lessons from a good instructor and if that's not possible buy an appropriate video. Casting is a very visual 'touchy feely' thing and it cannot always be learnt from a book especially if you have difficulty converting words to deeds.

Catch and Release

Catching and releasing your fish is commonplace in the US and widely accepted as the way to behave with trout. The practice is less widespread and probably more controversial in the UK. This is largely due to commercially stocked rainbow trout fisheries asking for dubious catch and release policies in order to maintain stock levels without the need to put more fish in. There is an air of pompous self-righteousness about putting back a stock pond fish, surely they are grown as a crop and not meant to be continuously put back into the same stew bowl. Ask the same angler if he would put back a goodly sized wild trout that had taken him days to catch rather than minutes and catch and release may not figure in his answer. Yet wild fish populations which are under threat from depleting numbers are just the ones that benefit from a flexible catch and release policy – flexible in the sense some wild trout populations can over burden themselves with numbers when the natural spawning is too prolific. This causes a fall in the average size of the trout when too many fish compete for the same amount of food. In this situation a catch and kill policy is better until the average size is upped again. There are also arguments put forward that the *barbless hooks* used in catch and release can cause excessive damage to the jaw of a trout as it spins around on the hook. The jury is still out on that argument.

Catch Returns

Where fisheries operate on a commercial basis you will often be asked to complete a catch return. These angling returns help in providing management with some guidance on future strategies on how to keep the fishery productive, whether it might need restocking or whether it needs 'resting' to allow naturally regenerating trout to recover their numbers. Although they sound like the perfect management tool, catch returns have significant drawbacks. Anglers can forget to give them back, fill them in only if they are successful or exaggerate sizes of fish caught to save face. Where catch and release operates in tandem with a catch and kill policy it is easy to tell a white lie and say he or she caught but returned a few more trout than was actually the case. Also unless there is a space for detailing *effort* i.e. the hours spent fishing in relation to the catch, the catch return is all but useless. Taking forty-eight hours to catch six trout is just not the same as forty-eight minutes to catch six of the best.

Cat's Whisker
The Cat's Whisker is an extremely popular pattern in the UK tied streamer style principally for stillwater rainbows. It is basically a deeper water fly fished fast on a sunk or intermediate line. Black or white marabou feather forms the main part of the wing tied over a green or yellow fluorescent chenille body and a red gloss head. Bead eyes are sometimes added to make the fly fish deeper. Some of the *Clouser* patterns from the USA closely resemble this UK pattern.

Caution (in Trout)
Cautious trout live longer. Fish which are reckless and bold are usually the ones we catch first. Some strains of trout exhibit more guarded *behaviour* than others. A classic example of this is the shy secretive wild brown trout as compared with the 'bold as brass' rainbow. When you catch a fish you have invoked a confident rather than a cautious response to your fly presentation. The secret of successful fishing is therefore not to spook trout when you cast to them, do that and you won't see the more canny ones for dust.

Characteristics of Brown Trout
In Britain during the Victorian era, natural historians gave trout glamorous names such as the 'Golden' trout or the 'Parr Marked' trout. While this was a nice idea it led to all sorts of unnecessary confusion about classification of species. Basically all brown trout now come under the genus *Salmo trutta* with little offshoots denoting differing strains such as *Leven* or *Ferox*. What the Victorians did get right was the recording of differing characteristics displayed by the trout, it was the wrong association of these qualities with different species which let them down. Traits in brown trout, for example the free rising roving athleticism of the silvery Leven trout, are an ingrained genetic adaptation to habitat. Equally some trout show much darker markings and flanks owing to the nature of their habitat, their colouration developed as camouflage. It is all in the *genes* and nothing to do with a different species but whatever it is the characteristics of brown trout are the thing that keeps us anglers coming back for more.

Children Fishing
Taking a child trout fishing is just about the best thing you could do but for goodness sake make it fun! Children have short attention spans; they need adventure, muddy puddles and wriggly trout. They don't need long

Fishing should be fun not an endurance test for children.

boring demonstrations of how wonderful your own casting is or lengthy tales of that monster trout you caught last week. Children want to experience it all for themselves with you there in the background to help and keep them safe. If the first trout they catch is only four inches they will still think it's the biggest to come from that stream and that's all that matters. A bit of guddling around in the shallows and seeing what the trout eats keeps the interest up as does a really good picnic. Fishing should be fun for everyone, it is not an endurance test.

Chironomids
Generic term for the family of flat-winged midges including black, green and red varieties and of course the pesky biting one so prevalent in boggy areas of the UK. Anglers in the UK will also refer to these as *buzzers* and with over three hundred varieties of chironomid in the British Isles that's an awful lot of buzzing.

Claret
The use of claret coloured materials for bodies or hackles of flies seems to be a peculiarly British thing. Few North American patterns seem to incorporate this colour. This is perhaps a pity as when it comes to fly composition the wine stain of claret is far more subtle than any bright red or solid black. Noted patterns in the UK using claret in their make up include the ubiquitous Grouse and Claret (see also *Grouse Winged Flies*), Mallard and Claret and the Claret *Bumble*. The claret materials used include claret seal's fur, wool and floss as well as hen hackles dyed to the appropriate shade.

Climate Change
Our overcrowded consumer world is overheating from the effects of modern consumerism. We guzzle gas, over exploit our Earth, pollute our atmosphere, create global warming and destabilise our environment. Trout habitat might seem a long way removed from this but it isn't really. Where once we had even flows of water in our rivers we now have more droughts or floods. In Scotland where once we had two months of snow and ice in winter in the 1950s and 60s we now have maybe three weeks if we are lucky, either that or it snows in June! Numerous other European countries are experiencing this type of alteration in their weather cycles. Climate change, particularly these increasingly common sudden swings between extremes of heat and cold, high or low water have a cruel effect on trout populations. Young trout are vulnerable to both droughts and *spates* and many mortalities occur when the natal stream condition alters. Trout in stillwaters do not escape either because for prolonged heatwaves cause a deoxygenation of water and/or an excessive growth of

algae all of which can ring the death knell for the fish inhabitants. This is a problem which won't go anyway but successive global governments shrug it off as if it isn't happening.

Clouds

Cloud cover helps no end in your fishing exploits. Brilliant cloudless skies are hard work when trying to catch trout. The best fishing conditions always involve a modicum of cloud. In the UK a grey overcast mild day with a breeze is one heck of a lot better than boiling humid sunshine. Though clouds mean no spooky shadows of anglers on the water to scare fish they also have the advantage of creating a semi uniform background of light which seems to make the trout see your fly better. Wild trout are light-sensitive creatures incapable of blinking (no eyelids!) and they will shy away from a direct bright light shining into their eyes. Cloud cover alleviates this problem. Seasoned anglers can interpret weather patterns through watching cloud formations. In basic terms high scattered white

The Clouser.

cloud means a fine day whereas low heavy grey clouds which seem to be gathering in intensity can signal rain and/or stormy weather.

Clousers
I was first introduced to this American fly by Ann and Ted Bounds in Arizona. Their particular version was a Coyote Clouser but it's a fly with many variations. It is an inverted hook pattern meant to imitate a small fleeing fish and was originally tied by Bob Clouser to catch smallmouth bass in Pennsylvania. According to John Gierach in his book *Good Flies*, Clousers are tied on straight-eyed stream hooks with lead eyes at the top of the shank. The usual colours of these eyes are red or yellow with a black pupil but nowadays variants are legion. Similarly, the body was usually made of bucktail in a variety of colours (olive, pink or tan and silver are favourites) however today just about anything goes. Clousers were meant to imitate *crawdads* or Mud Bugs depending on which part of the US you hail from. The action of a Clouser in water is very distinctive as the fly actually swims deep and upside down with a rise and fall between retrieves. It is meant for bumping along on or very near the bottom and the inverted hook helps it not to get snagged. UK semi equivalents almost exclusively used in rainbow rather than brown trout fishing would be *lures* like the eyed Cat's Whisker, Dog Nobbler or the Damsel Nymph.

Clunker
A peculiarly Scottish word for a large fish. If you have lost a 'clunker' you have lost something special in the way of a trout. There is an old English word 'lunker' which means the same thing but is not much used these days, anyway being a Scot I think clunker is much more descriptive!

Clyde Style Flies
In Scotland the River Clyde has a long illustrious history of fishing. Many pioneering doyens of Scottish river angling enjoyed their time there in the 1800s and being so near the main cities of Glasgow and Edinburgh it remains a hugely popular venue. A number of now traditional wet and dry fly patterns first found favour there. Clyde anglers devised a particular style of fly construction with sparse dressings featuring a distinctive upright wing tied at a steep angle to the body. This style may have been devised to imitate the big hatches of March Browns, Olives and Iron Blues found on this river but in the days of flimsy *horsehair* the bold wings may have been constructed to give the fly extra wind resistance and send it out over the water further with a following wind. Noted Clyde style patterns still in use today include the Yellow May, Sand Fly and Dark Spring Olive.

Clyde Style Flies.

Coch Y Bondhu

A supremely useful wet fly coming out of the Welsh school of fly tying. The Coch Y Bondhu is a beetle (also known as a Bracken Clock in Scotland) and the imitation does indeed have a beetle shape. However this fly can be used with confidence for just about any fat bodied insect on the water and indeed will take trout feeding almost exclusively on freshwater *shrimps* such is its versatility. The dressing is simplicity itself with a peacock herl body, red game (furnace) hackle with black centre and black tips, optional tag of gold tinsel. A rib of fine gold wire can be used for extra weight. The use of the more subtle two tone pale brown and black hackle increases the trout attraction rate of this fly considerably.

Colouration in Trout

Trout have the most amazing variation in colours and markings. Even in one localised population all emanating from the same natural spawning redds you will find a complex mix of colours and markings. Distinctive colours of a particular trout population can sometimes but not always indicate a distinct strain, see also *characteristics*. A lot of trout colouration stems from the need to develop camouflage for the immediate environment, trout in dark water tend to be naturally dark golden brown while trout in pale limpid green water have more silver colours. It's a question of self preservation, blending in is better than sticking out a mile.

A rich golden brown safely in the net.

Competition amongst Trout

Competition for basic elements of survival like finding food and securing a mate can be a major source of stress for trout. Trout much prefer a quiet life to a cut and thrust competitive one. Serious battles for *stations*, shelter and food are common amongst small trout from fry stage to around maturity. Once the trout have gained sufficient body weight to stand up to their brethren and/or predators, and they have managed to establish their own territory however small, then life improves a little. However there is still plenty of action if one trout strays into a bigger fish's territory or tries to muscle in on the natural process of procreation. Fights between male trout are common as they compete to win their place beside the females and fertilise their eggs. Precocious fry can sometimes slip in and shed milt on the eggs while the bigger males are engaged in barging each other off the redds. Kind of like humans really…

Competition Angling

Competitive angling seems always to inspire heated debate. There are those who argue that angling competitions deface the value of the easy going enjoyment of a gentle sport in a tranquil environment. Conversely competitive fishers say they are answering the ultimate challenge of trying to catch fish 'to order' whatever the conditions might be doing at the time. Not surprisingly these diverse views cause friction, sometimes justified sometimes not. Where competitions become so intense they lead to unsavoury rivalry to the point of sectarianism, the beauty of the gentle art seems rather lost. However if there is a good natured camaraderie amongst the competitors and ideas and information exchanged without grudge, then there is little harm in it.

Concealment

The need to conceal your intentions when trying to catch trout is obvious however you would be surprised how many forget this simple tactic in the heat of a *rise*. On a river, to aid concealment try to keep your body below the horizon. Standing bolt upright on a bare bank shows your whole threatening shape to a fish below. Instead keep low and try to cast so as not to have your body higher than the surroundings. Fishing on stillwaters, try to keep the contours of the bank higher than your profile, in a boat keep low and avoid standing up for safety as much as concealment.

Condition

The condition of a trout can be judged by its shape, feel and colour. Out of condition trout can be thin bodied, slightly floppy with larger heads than normal particularly after spawning. Equally trout can be in poor fettle when ready to spawn being coated in extra mucous, darker in colour than normal and the females have their bellies swollen with eggs. Spawning males have big heads and *kypes* and may extrude milt when handled. Trout under stress from polluted water can feel slimy and somewhat limp with a coat of extra thick mucous developed to try and give added protection from pollution. Fish in prime condition show good proportion, have bright bold colours, firm flesh with a normal mucous coat.

Conditions

In trout fishing, for conditions read weather. Trout generally react much faster than us to any change in the prevailing conditions. Fish are much more tuned in to nature and their very survival can depend on it. Changes in light and temperature have a direct bearing on how trout react. For example brilliant sunshine literally 'blinds' fish and your fly may be much more difficult for them to spot. Dark cloudy skies make for easier vision in fish. Warm air makes better feeding conditions bringing on insect hatches while cold temperatures can have the opposite effect. Anglers will often describe the best conditions as grey, warm and with a breeze but not a fearsome gale.

Cormorants

Many large inland waters in the UK are plagued by the greedy fish-eating sea cormorant. Unfortunately legislation has been passed protecting these birds, which means that these pests are largely free to invade territory where they do not normally reside. Because the feeding is that much better in sheltered inland waters, especially stocked trout lakes, the cormorant has become wise to these easier pickings. Why ride out the winter in wild seas and crashing waves when a nice user-friendly lake offers a much softer option! Culling by shooting can only be done by complicated licensing. As is the case with *seals* this seems a short-sighted view totally at odds with the reality of pest control.

Cowdung Flies

Though these natural terrestrial insects emanate from the most unsavoury of places the trout love them. Wind-blown cow dung flies landing on the water by the bus load send fish into a frenzy of feeding every bit as good as any olive hatch. The cowdung looks like a bright gold yellow housefly and the Golden Olive *Bumble* makes an excellent imitation.

Crawdads

Crawdads are small crayfish found in the mud of USA rivers and lakes and are also sometimes referred to as mud bugs. The *Clouser* is one of the most used imitations for a crawdad. Crayfish imitations in the UK are not particularly common, any big *lure* like a Dog Nobbler will usually do the job.

Creek

In the US, creeks are small streams also known as burns in Scotland. Size is deceptive however for some apparently minute creeks hold some remarkably big trout. Creek fishing is exciting and demanding and requires a delicate *presentation* in miniature surroundings. A variety of tactics can be employed, usually imitative fishing catches more trout but *Streamers* can also be used. Upstream dry and nymph fishing is probably the most popular in creeks.

Creel

Traditionally, creels are the best way of transporting trout. Made of interwoven wicker they allow air to pass through and stop the smelly mess our modern tackle bags sometimes become. Anglers of old would often talk of 'filling the creel' as the result of a good day's trouting. The use of creels has slowly receded with lighter more modern materials taking their place.

Cruising Fish

If you espy a cruising trout then you may be in for a treat. Interception is the key as a trout which is actively roving his territory is on the lookout for food morsels coming his way. It is sometimes assumed that brown trout are solitary territorial creatures not given to going on the prowl. If a luscious food supply is constantly drifting down on its nose then this may well be the case. However because of changing *conditions* the food sources may alter or dry up altogether meaning the trout has to become more active and cruise around in search of food. If the hatch is abundant then the fish become greedy and stray from their normal stations to snap up the extra morsels. This is when trout make themselves more vulnerable, a feeding fish is a taking one. Get your fly in the trout's cruising path and there is a good chance he or she will take it providing your cast has been delicate and true.

Crustaceans

Trout love to munch on freshwater crustaceans and why not as these mainly bottom-hugging creepy crawlies are a wonderful source of protein. Shrimps, crayfish and water slaters (also known as hoglice) are the crustaceans most commonly consumed by trout. Shrimps of the Gammarus family are common in alkaline based waters of both the UK and the US. Crayfish are common only to specific UK waters while water slaters are not the first choice for trout, they much prefer a shrimp diet to a slater one. Daphnia (tiny water fleas) are sometimes classed as crustaceans and trout will avidly follow clouds of daphnia as they rise and fall according to daylight hours. A good guide to water quality is to look in the shallows for the larger, easier seen, crustacean populations like shrimp, if the water is very acid they will not exist and consequently trout growth rates may be slower and fish smaller. Trout with a high crustacean content in their diet have rich red/pink flesh and make very good eating.

Shrimp imitations are legion either as exact replicas or as vague traditional patterns. In Scotland one of the most popular shrimp imitation is a Soldier Palmer which has a brown palmered hackle, red body and gold rib. Interestingly the natural shrimp can sometimes be found bespeckled with an orange (carotene) or blue dot and therefore imitations with these colours present – such as the Orange Invicta – do well when the trout are shrimp gulping. Crayfish in the UK can grow to a threatening size especially the marauding alien signal crayfish. These nasty monsters are more likely to consume small trout than the other way round. Crayfish imitations in the US are discussed under *Clousers*.

Cul de Canard CDC

Cul de Canard or CDC is one of the most effective feathers ever to be used in dry fly construction. It comes from the feathers on the behind of a duck

Cul de Canard CDC flies.

hence the slang 'duck's bum' description. This is marvellously water
repellent material. Its advantages over other lesser hackles are its delicate
semi-transparent subtle qualities which leave other feathers standing. Just
a few strands are enough to ensure a buoyant extremely life-like fly.
Popular European CDC imitations include the CDC Midge, CDC Emerger,
CDC Hopper and CDC Sedge and these are successful on both flowing and
still water. It does not appear to be in so much use in the US yet but give it
time, nothing comes as close as this in natural imitation.

Current

In any river or stream the current will dictate how a trout behaves. It's the
bringer of food as well as less pleasant effects like upstream pollution. The
bigger more dominant trout tend to hold the best *stations* in the current.
These will normally be just off the main flow with easy access to food and
shelter from predators. When water levels fall during periods of drought
the current slows and trout seek any faster streamy runs in order to
maximise oxygen over their gills. Conversely in high water trout may seek
shelter at the sides of the stream to save on energy. Battling to hold
station in a fast tearaway current is hard work and trout will always seek a
happy medium.

Cute Factor

Unlike some of its main predators notably the *seal*, trout do not possess
that magic cute factor which would grant them some extra protection
from the ravages of the modern industrial world. Even though trout have
been occasionally favourably mentioned throughout classic English
literature other than in angling writings, they remain a largely ignored
creature hidden away in their aquatic habitat. This places them at an
immediate disadvantage when it comes to holistic conservation measures.
In the UK, the pretty-faced fish predator the common grey seal or the
visually attractive fish eating bird the Great Northern Diver, will always
gain the public sympathy vote way before the unseen trout. Anglers may
rave over the beauty and colour of the wild trout they have just caught but
to the vast majority of the general public, fish are cold slimy things with
little or no cuddly bunny appeal.

Cutthroat Trout

A beautifully marked American indigenous trout recognised by a
characteristic reddish orange flash across the gill cover. The Cutthroat has
a long evolutionary history splitting into distinct sub species including
coastal and westslope forms. Distinctive Cutthroat populations also exist
in places like Yellowstone and Montana. Hybridisation with other trout
and destruction of native habitats has led to a decline in rare populations.

Plans are now set in motion to protect and preserve this native American trout and hopefully these will allow anglers to enjoy the athletic Cutthroat for a little while longer.

Czech Nymphs

Probably first invented (remember everything in fishing has been done before!) by the Czech international fishing team. In order to assist nymphs to sink quickly in fast water, heavy metal-like tungsten or lead was applied at the head and/or around the body of the nymph. The result is a weighty ungainly thing indeed, however, the results from Czech nymphing can be quite spectacular especially in difficult high water. The nymph is lobbed upstream and then allowed to trundle down toward you on a short line with a high raised rod tip. Anglers watch the nylon for tweaks from trout and strike immediately there is any movement. Unless tied in very small dressings it is not easy to cast these types of nymphs, a roll cast is the most common method. Superb for deeper water fishing but not everyone's cup of tea as the technique is rather like upstream worming. It all depends on your desperation to catch fish.

Daddies

In the UK if you fish a 'Daddy' you are fishing an imitation of a crane fly, a relatively large but very skinny legged insect which hatches on land at certain times of year, notably August. It is an insect indigenous to most parts of Britain and the trout go mad when a cluster of these are blown on to the water. On its day 'Daddy' fishing can be every bit as exciting as angling during the *mayfly* hatch. There are some pretty neat dressings size 8 to 12 for this incongruous insect, some anglers prefer the realistic knotted leg variety with a beefy body and splayed wings. Others go for a more general representation like a French Partridge. Either way these big flies can be fished semi static or twitched with spectacular effect during Daddy time. *Hoppers* are smaller versions of the well dressed mouthful and these are fished *top of the water style* with a faster retrieve.

Dams

Dams placed over freshwater systems for whatever reason are usually a curse to all fish that reside there. Whether it is electricity generation or whether it is to create a reservoir of drinking water, anything that unnaturally alters the flow of a river or the height of a lake spells a change in trout habitat. An even flow of water is fine but when you artificially raise levels of water above the dam and artificially lower water levels below it, trout can find previously productive feeding areas completely submerged or dried out depending on their location. Water abstraction from dams also suddenly alters the quality of feeding and where there is also wind and wave action on the lake, bare eroded habitats result along the shoreline. Water abstraction also dries up spawning areas and this results in a loss of future generations of trout. In the UK it is now a legal offence to block the passage of migratory fish (non migratory fish like brown trout are ignored), dams must have fish passes on them. However that is too late to correct the damage down by the great hydro electric schemes of the 1950s which irrevocably altered some of Britain's finest wild fish waters.

Damsel Flies
Damsel flies are relatively large skinny-legged insects common throughout the UK. They bear a close resemblance to their bigger cousins the Dragon

A French damsel fly alights on vegetation.

fly. The natural insect is quite spectacular occurring as the Large Red damsel or the Common Blue damsel. Both are delicate-winged and brightly coloured. Damsels are normally found in and around lakes and slower flowing rivers but are occasionally blown off course to turn up in people's gardens. Usually the natural insect emerges in the summer months when light and warmth first hit the water. Damsel nymphs crawl out and hatch on reed or plant stems at the water's edge hence it is sometimes wrongly assumed that they are purely land-born insects. The flight of a damsel alternates between fast and hovering and once airborne it is not easy prey for a fish. The bottom-crawling nymphs of damsels however are eagerly eaten by trout and many anglers do not bother with a representation of the hatched version simply using a sunk nymph pattern. Dressings for this nymph vary from plump bodied yellow/gold nymphs to marabou fringed versions which look remarkably like that US favourite the *Clouser*.

Dance
A number of natural insects including mayfly, larger midges and olives have a ritualistic fluttering dance airborne at the sides of the water before mating. If you see this dance going on when you arrive at your favourite water then you must be on your mettle for there is no doubt the trout have noticed it too and will be enjoying its bounty. Dancing columns of flies rising and falling in small clouds above bushes and/or below trees are a clear indication a significant hatch is going on.

Daphnia
Daphnia are those millions of microscopic creatures such as water fleas which inhabit freshwater lakes. Scientists will refer to them as zooplankton but anglers more often than not speak of daphnia feeding trout. Daphnia migrate in clouds up toward the surface on dull days and or in the evenings. In times of brilliant sun, they head back down to the depths. This movement means that trout can follow daphnia in an obsessive manner unless there is larger more easily accessible prey like mayfly or sedge available. Daphnia feeding fish are not impossible to catch despite there being no imitation of the real thing. Interception at the right depth is the key and a large garish fly with orange or green in its make-up will often work. A Teal and Green, Dunkeld or Orange Invicta are often useful. A feeding trout is a taking trout no matter what it happens to be consuming.

Dapping
Dapping is an ancient angling art found principally in the UK on lochs and big lakes. It harks back to the earliest days of fishing with connotations of

the Mediterranean *Bolognese rods* and more recently greenheart rods and horsehair lines. With dapping the angler does not so much cast as hold the rod aloft and let the wind blow out the line and fly forward toward the waiting trout. Modern dapping rods are telescopic affairs anything from 11ft up to 16ft in length. A normal floating line can be used on the reel with a lengthy 'leader' of light dapping floss. Some dapping aficionados recommend using floss straight on to braided backing but you need a separate reel and a heck of a lot of backing and floss to fill the reel drum. The floss line must be of sufficient length to be hoisted skyward and allowed to waft about naturally in the wind. Right at the sharp end of the floss is a short nylon leader with a large dapping fly attached. Dapping flies are heavily dressed mouthfuls size 8/10 'Badgers' and 'Black Palmers' being favourites though a size 10 French Partridge will do at a pinch. The technique is simple, hold the rod up and let the floss billow forward allowing the fly to dap upon the water surface. This makes the fly look like a struggling insect trying to escape and can theoretically attract fish. Great if fish are seeing it but deathly boring if nothing is happening as no casting is involved. It is common for gillies worried about one of their guest's ability to cast from a boat to give them a dapping rod which they only need to point skyward while the other guests cast with a normal fly line – keeps everyone out of harm's way! Dapping with live *mayfly* and *daddies* is popular in Ireland and some stillwaters in northern Scotland however if the trout are taking well a fat artificial works just as well.

Dark Olive

The large dark olive forms an essential part of the river trout's menu. It is a common upright winged delicate insect found in most rivers and streams in the UK with the main hatches occurring in the Spring. It probably has a natural American equivalent, certainly it's an olive worth imitating wherever it is found. In the UK hatches can occur early on around midday while in May hatches of large dark olives are more common at dusk. Semi-traditional imitations are along the lines of Greenwell's Glory, Wickham's Fancy or Kite's Imperial while more modern fly fishers might want to use a size 14 CDC or an Adams. As dark olives are members of the wide ranging *olive* family, the nymphs are also readily taken by trout. Most olive nymph imitations in the Hare's Ear vein do the trick. In the US, John Gierach gives a dressing for a Speckled Spinner in his book *Good Flies* and with its mottled grey partridge wing and body of stripped natural blue dun quill, olive dubbed thorax and two tails it looks just like a dark olive to British trout.

Deer Hair

At one time just about the only fly in the UK using deer hair was a big

Deer hair head on a Castag fly from Northern Scotland.

Muddler Minnow, now there are numerous variations some it has to be said more subtle than others. Mini Muddlers with smaller trimmings led the charge and today many British anglers use these along with American patterns made using bucktail or elk hair. The advantages of including deer hair in a fly dressing include its water repellence factor which makes the end result very buoyant. For this reason deer hair is often used in 'wake' flies which create a disturbance on the water surface akin to a scuttering *Sedge*. Deer hair has some disadvantages however as it is a difficult and frustrating material to work with at the vice and in the hands of an amateur fly dresser the end result can be an appallingly bulbous mess. Also there is the problem of cautious trout who wish to knock/stun the natural fly down and take it safely beneath the surface where they are less exposed to predators. Deer hair patterns can make this fishy tactic impossible as it keeps popping back up and consequently trout are sometimes spooked by this odd behaviour.

Dibble

Dapping and dibbling are sometimes thought to be the same method of working a fly however while dapping employs its own special rod and floss

Dibbling a fly on Loch Watten, Caithness, Scotland.

tackle, dibbling is mainly concerned with a tactic employed in *loch style* fishing. This type of traditional angling has its roots in the nineteenth century but is still very popular today. It employs a floating line and a team of flies on *droppers*. During the lift off the rod tip will be raised to allow the top dropper to 'dibble' across the water surface before the line is aerialised again. This makes the fly dance on the water surface akin to a natural insect taking flight and every now and again a trout will make a smash and grab take at it. Dibbling is best carried out from a boat although it can also be done from the bank providing there is a reasonable breeze.

Disc

Disc or disc drag is the clever part of the internal workings of a fly reel which controls the speed at which the line goes out and is retrieved. The design is basic with two serrated discs/wheels which fit together at different settings to adjust a little spring lever. On the outside of the reel drum there is a plus and minus switch which allows the angler to alter the disc drag of the reel. Set high on the plus scale the fly line is effectively braked and slowed in running out when a heavy fish takes. Put way down on the minus setting the line is easily run off the drum and therefore it is quite possible for a big trout to whip you down to the backing before you know it. Anglers sometimes fail to make use of the disc drag in the heat of battle so it is advisable to check that it is set on a happy medium between plus and minus before starting fishing.

Distance

Some anglers become obsessed with distance casting perhaps believing the trout are always just out of reach. Mighty macho lines are launched into the blue yonder, power casting at its best. Competitions will be held to see who casts the longest line and prizes won and lost. Sadly while it might look impressive to the uninitiated, distance casting will only help you catch fish if the trout happen to be out there in the first place. Too many fishermen ignore the fact that trout like to lie next to food and shelter and there may not be too much of that 30 yards offshore in deep open water. In his obsessive relentless effort to reach that fabulous distance, the angler will often have *lined* i.e. disturbed and put down as many as half a dozen trout in the process. Nevertheless a whole tackle culture has grown up around the ability to cast huge distances with lines and rods manufactured with the sole intent of going further. Fishermen should also remember that even if you hit on a trout far out with such a lot of loose line extended from the reel you have a reduced chance of hooking your fish successfully. In effect you are relying on the trout hooking itself rather than your ability to *strike* quickly.

Distribution of Trout

On any freshwater system trout will usually be distributed along or around it according to territorial need and genetic influences. The bigger stronger trout will be distributed nearest to the best sources of food and have easily accessible bolt holes from predators. Lesser trout in the pecking order will nearly always be distributed in the poorer territories with less good feeding and cover. Ancient strains of trout distributed during the retreat of the last ice age may well develop genetic characteristics which allow them to survive in their particular patch. Unfortunately our obsession for stocking both rivers and lakes with additional trout from different colonies has meant that the original distribution of trout across the northern and southern hemisphere has been irrevocably altered especially when the introduced fish have interbred with the native species.

Double Hander

Double handed rods are principally employed in salmon angling and have only a minor but nevertheless important role in the capture of trout. If you are a right hander fishing a windswept water where the gale is blasting straight on to your right shoulder, you might well wish you could cast over your left side without crossing the rod over the body. A small *butt* extension which effectively makes your rod into a double hander allows you to cast on both sides with equal grace. Perhaps not in the best tradition of single handed trout fly rods but nevertheless mighty useful when the wind blows hard from the wrong direction. Various rod manufacturers now add a small butt extension which protects the reel seat when it is stood up on the ground but at a pinch you can use this as part of a double hander. In extreme weather conditions it is better to be adaptable rather than packing up and going home.

Double Haul

In the UK tournament casters frequently use a casting method known as the double haul. This technique is also used for extra distance off the bank especially when fishing for stocked rainbows. It involves aerialising a huge amount of line by a series of tweaks and pulls before the whole caboodle is shot forward. Double hauling is not a method to be learned by the printed word, if you want to acquire this skill go to a qualified instructor. It will add yards to your cast but there is still no guarantee that the trout are that far out or that you will be able to get a firm hook hold 40 yards away!

Doubles (Wee)

You might think this refers to a shot of whisky but in the UK, wee doubles are actually trout and sea trout flies tied on a double rather than a single hook. They are very successful in situations which call for a deeper sunk fly. The normal tactic is to put the wee double (something like a Dunkeld or an Invicta) on the leader point and then have lighter *droppers* above. The extra weight of this fly pulls the leader down quickly and trout either take the double or the droppers suspended higher than it. This type of fly has strong associations with catching trout on Loch *Leven* where at one time it was considered a highly useful tactic. Today it is still in use but is less popular due to other inventions like the heavy *Czech nymphs*.

Dour

Dour is a wonderful old Scots word meaning that there is little action going on. It can be used to describe fish activity i.e. 'The trout are dour today' or it can be employed in describing a particular water as in 'This loch is very dour'. The very mention of this word can bring a passing frown to the brow of even the most fervent optimist as it means there are tough times ahead. However it should be noted that dour waters often hold a monster trout or two and you might just get lucky.

Drag

In fishing there are two meanings to the term drag. The first concerns the little switch or screw on the side of your reel which when adjusted allows the line to be pulled off faster or slower. Setting the correct drag is important if you are playing big fish. The second meaning concerns dry fly fishing on rivers. When a dry fly skates unnaturally across the surface too fast it is called drag. Drag occurs when the current has got a real hold on your line bellying it forward in front of the fly. This causes the fly and leader to be whipped across or down the stream so quickly the artificial ends up looking incongruously awkward. Flies which are dragging in the current more times than they are floating at a natural pace can scare trout and put them down. The key to avoiding drag is careful line control with gentle *mending* to make sure you stay in touch with your dry fly but at the same time not allowing it to appear unnatural. Drag is not all bad news however as some trout find the wake it makes attractive especially if they are sea trout which love to chase down their prey. Equally in stillwaters, flies which drag in the wind make a wake which can stimulate an aggressive take, see also *dibble*.

Drake(s)

The term Drake is primarily associated with mayfly as in 'Green Drakes' and to a much lesser extent 'Grey' or 'Black Drakes'. There is also a school of thought which associates the traditional use of feathers from the mallard duck (drake) in the making of the wings of the artificial fly and therefore this was how the fly got its name. Through time in the UK the upright winged hatched stage of the *mayfly* (*Ephemera danica* or *Ephemera vulgata*) has become associated with the term drake thus distinguishing it from the smaller olives. Imitations of Drakes are legion in the UK stretching right back to the days of F M Halford. Mayfly Duns and Mayfly Spinner imitations are probably the best known and easily recognised by their long bodies and three long tails. The Americans rather confusingly call every variety of the olive family a mayfly and there are a number of flies involving Drake in the title for example the Parachute Green Drake or the Brown Drake Emerger. However as trout are the final judge of a pattern, as long as it works perhaps we should not be too pedantic about its name.

Dressing

The dressing of a fly is all the components of fur, silk and feather which go into its make up. How to dress a fly will also involve the way in which

The Mayfly Drake.

these components are to be applied to the hook for example a 'sparse' dressing differs from a 'heavy' one. There is a certain historical romance to the term dressing a fly as it is deeply instilled in all forms of fly tying. One of the earliest testimonies to it is in *Northern Memoirs* by R Franck, written circa 1694, which states 'And among the variety of your fly adventurers, remember the hackle, or the fly substitute formed without wings and drest [dressed] up with the feather of a capon, pheasant or partridge...' Today there are thousands of dressings/patterns for flies world-wide.

Drift

In trout fishing if you enjoy a good drift it is not necessarily because you have just smoked a funny cigarette but more that you have just drifted down a shore in a boat and cast to some good trout on the way. The best drifts are almost always across productive fishy areas, sections of a stillwater holding good food and good cover for trout. Drifts are set by the way the wind is blowing that day and with local knowledge to hand it is likely you will be drifting toward a fish hot spot near or parallel to the shore. Drifts across deep open water are not normally very productive as the trout are usually holed up in the more fertile margins. However in uniformly shallow lakes, lochs or loughs, a drift across open water can be undertaken with confidence. Setting a drift and keeping to it is sometimes more difficult than it looks especially if the boat is light and keeps turning awkwardly. A *drogue* trailing out behind from mid ships slows the progress down sufficiently to allow anglers to cast forward with the wind behind. Traditionally the best drift is always side on to the wind so that the two or three occupants of the boat can cast at fish rising in front of them.

Drogue

Drogues are wonderful things to have attached to the boat in a high wind. They resemble a water filled parachute on a longish piece of rope which once dropped over the side acts as a sort of a free slow-moving anchor. Without a drogue in a gale the boat will move so fast that line retrieving becomes almost impossible for the angler. Putting out the drogue allows a more comfortable passage and gives the boat a little more stability in the bouncing waves. Always make sure the drogue is firmly attached amidships perhaps around a seat stem or duckboards. Once it becomes submerged it exerts quite a pulling force and if not tied on properly will easily be lost forever in the deeps.

Dropper(s)

In Scottish *loch style* fishing teams of flies are often employed. These are tied along the leader on short 6 to 8 inch droppers. The droppers are spaced anything up to about 6ft apart especially when it is essential to make the attached flies look unrelated. Ready-made leaders with droppers already attached can be purchased but this gives no flexibility in the space between the fly attachments. Many anglers prefer to make their own droppers straight on to a length of nylon. A simple figure of eight knot places the dropper on to the main length of nylon just where you want it. It is important the dropper is made of a fairly firm density nylon otherwise it will collapse and wind itself around the main line. In the 1800s in the UK, flies were simply tied into the main leader without droppers and this was known as a 'strap'. Up to twelve flies could be thus employed but with the invention of droppers this number fell to three or four.

Dry Fly

Though it was not always made obvious, the dry fly was invented many centuries after the wet. While wet flies had been around since the 1400s or earlier, the dry 'floating' fly only came into being in the mid to late 1800s. No single angler can be accredited with its invention, however England's F M Halford, circa 1880s, took the dry fly by the horns and drove it rapidly into cult status. Halford and his followers brought a considerable amount of unnecessary elitism often known as 'purism', to the gentle art. Halfordians declared that to catch a trout by any means other than a dry fly cast upstream of a fish and allowed to drift down on the current, was in effect cheating. To the *purist*, wet patterns fished across and down was a poor man's method executed using gross overdressed second class imitations. Dry flies were to be made and used to exactly represent local natural insects and in this respect we still today follow roughly that prescription. Thankfully now we generally take a less narrow view of our fishing using dry or wet fly according to the conditions. While in the twenty-first century the list of dry fly favourites in the UK and the US is now several miles long, patterns that have really stood the test of time include the Adams, the Rough Olive, Grey Wulff, dry Greenwell's Glory and the dry March Brown.

Dubbing

During the construction of a fly it is often necessary to use dubbing to make the appropriate shape of body. To do this you need to wax the tying thread to make it a little sticky then apply a small amount of seal's fur or similar in a gentle twisting motion around the thread using you thumb and index finger. Effective dubbing just makes the tying thread that bit thicker and the end result should be an insect body shape secured round the hook without the need for any more tying in. Picking out some of the dubbing fibres is often done with a dubbing needle when a more hairy/leggy body is required. Typical patterns employing dubbing include the Soldier Palmer or the Invicta.

Duck Fly

In Ireland early hatches of black midge or *buzzers* are known as duck fly. These hatches are profuse on the big loughs and many anglers will travel to Ireland simply to enjoy the sport in April and early May. Because this hatch is probably the prelude to the lush mayfly hatch of late May and June the trout come on the feed for duck fly and stay there. The best known imitation for duck fly is probably the Connemara Black with greyish wing, dark body and blue throat.

Dunkeld

The Dunkeld is a traditional UK/Scottish fly developed in the late 1800s. It has connotations of a *lure* constructed to vaguely imitate a small fleeing fish. Its bright orange hackle, gold body and jungle cock wings make it similar to some salmon fly dressings indeed it is as useful for sea trout as it is for browns. A combination of a Dunkeld as the *point fly* and a bushy top *dropper* can give the impression of a small fish chasing an attractive prey. Larger trout may seize the top dropper as a way of asserting their authority, a sort of 'I'm first in the food chain' reaction. Equally they might just smash into the Dunkeld as a way of seeing off the opposition. Either way you will have connected with an angry trout. Dressings vary between all orange including the wing to the traditional darker speckled brown mallard wing and jungle cock 'eyes'.

Dun(s)

The term dun is a corruption of the old Scots Gaelic word 'donn' meaning a darkish colour of brown. However fishermen often call upright winged insects duns when they have just emerged from the nymph stage but have not yet become a mature adult. A considerable number of fly imitations have dun in their title for example Pale Watery Dun, Olive Dun, Claret Dun and so on. The original Dun Fly goes way back to the days of the *Treatise* when it was described as having a dun body and partridge wing. Interestingly the term dun also appears in American descriptions of flies so it is now a universal one.

Early Fishing

'Early' fishing for trout is quality time at the beginning of the new season. Brown trout fishing in the UK is by law carried out between 15 March to 6 October with slight local variations. This close season was only introduced in the mid 1900s as a way of allowing the trout to spawn (late October to early December) and then recover. The bulk of the UK's early fishing therefore takes place in March and April, once May is reached we are into serious Spring, June to August constitute Summer fishing and September provides Autumn angling. While early season trouting is viewed to be too cold an affair by some, it still has a devoted band of followers. This is because there is always the likelihood of a larger than average trout being caught napping after the winter. All you need is a warm window in the weather and the fish will come on the take albeit for a short period. There is also something very special about fishing a water for the first time that year reliving old dramas and raising expectations for what is yet to come.

Ears

The ears of trout are hidden inside the head and are mainly concerned with balance though they are also able to detect some vibrations in the surrounding aquatic environment. Though you might think it in terms of the fish's ability to flee as you approach, a trout's ear is not as sophisticated as a human one. You can shout and screech to your buddy beside the water and the trout will not hear you, however stamp your feet and/or wave your arms around and they will almost certainly turn tail. Most detection of vibration in the water is done by the trout's highly sensitive lateral line which runs along the length of the fish's body. The lateral line acts almost as an echo sounder and warns the fish of approaching obstacles. It is if you like, the trout's third ear.

Eastern Flies
In the USA there is a subtle difference between flies made in the Eastern States and those tied on the Western seaboard. Basically flies used locally in the East are more delicate and can bear more resemblance to those of the English chalkstreams. Of course there is now much more crossing over of concepts but its worth pointing out this difference, see also *Western flies*.

Educated Trout
This is an odd phrase still in use today often used to describe cautious, difficult to catch trout. It probably emanates from the 1800s when the cult of dry fly took off. Trout caught on dry fly were portrayed as intellectually superior to trout caught on wet as were the trout of rivers as compared to stillwaters. This seemed to rather mirror the anglers' opinions of themselves, dry fly river fishing was at that time considered considerably superior to wet fly loch fishing, almost a class thing and not a welcome one. Sadly 'educated' trout have never existed rather the fish are creatures of considerable instincts for self preservation. Trout have a brain about the size of a lentil and have no intellectual capacity whatsoever however caution is their watchword and that is how they survive.

Effort
When fishermen report on their day's catch it is interesting to see how much attention they pay to effort i.e. the amount of time spent thrashing the water as compared to the end result. Catching two trout in twenty-four hours is simply not the same as hooking a couple in less than an hour. *Catch returns* must have a section which relates the effort expended to the final tally, without this they are pretty meaningless. Sadly even when time spent fishing is recorded, vanity can take over and anglers can become economical with the truth as to how long it actually took them to catch that trout of their dreams. For this reason the old style fishing logs which give total bag, largest fish and weather

conditions sometimes fail to give a true picture of the productivity of a fishery.

Eggs (Imitations)

All trout will happily consume salmon and trout eggs which have been shifted off the redds in high water. They are a neat blob of protein being trundled down on the current and few fish will resist such an easy mouthful. In the UK a variety of patterns have been designed to imitate eggs and these include Glo Bugs, Krystal Eggs and Blobs. All are simply a ball of brightly coloured material wound around a hook to form an egg shape. Purist they ain't but in times of fast water spates they are remarkably effective if fished in tandem with a heavy nymph pattern.

Eggs of Trout

Mature female brown trout usually begin to produce eggs in Spring which then increase in size and volume through summer until the eggs are full sized. Once ready to spawn the female will show a swollen distended belly and if caught in this condition eggs will sometimes extrude from her body. The lady should be returned immediately and allowed to finish the business of continuation of the species. Spawning will then take place in late Autumn and early Winter when the male will fertilise the eggs on the redds. Different trout species will spawn at different times, for example rainbows reproduce at different times from browns. The number of eggs a female trout produces varies according to her length, age and body weight. Anything from two hundred to over two thousand eggs will grow within her lower body cavity on follicles however the aquatic environment can temper the number of eggs produced with highly acid waters sometimes leading to poorer egg production. Female trout may naturally vary in fecundity which in turn can place a particular trout strain under threat of extinction, however given a chance nature usually manages to strike a balance.

Elasticity

Trout populations worldwide exhibit elasticity, that is an ability to only grow to a size their resident water will sustain. Thus if you take the average 9in trout from deep often acidic upland waters and deposit it in a rich fertile shallow alkaline environment they will grow much larger. This elasticity will not happen overnight as genetic influences regarding growth rates can come into play, nevertheless monsters can be nurtured from mini trout. In the UK this practice was at one time common on Scottish highland estates, less so now, when small trout were moved from tiny burns (streams) and planted out in bigger lochs where the natural spawning was poor. They would then be left for a year or so and on return the trout would have grown considerably, making a fine catch for the lateral thinking angler.

Elk Hair

In the US the use of elk hair in dry fly patterns has been going on for many years however the UK has only cottoned on to this buoyant material within the last twenty years or so. Elk hair is a little easier to work with than deer hair being slightly more pliant. Its colour too is often a paler shade of brown adding a degree more subtlety to the pattern. Common flies employing elk hair include the Elk Hair Caddis, Elk Hair Humpy, Elk Hair Sedge, Cahill Quill and Light Caddis. Flies incorporating elk hair are equally at home on either flowing or stillwater and they are extremely versatile for vague representations of most winged insects.

Emerging Insects

All aquatic bred insects go through a transition phase from nymph to mature hatched insect. This phase of shedding their nymph form and beginning a new life as a winged insect is called emerging. It will normally take place on the water surface just in the surface film and insects can be seen struggling to wriggle out of nymph shucks and emerge on to the water, a process which takes only a few seconds. The trout quickly pick up when there are emergers on the water and will feed avidly on this vulnerable plunder.

Ephemera

Ephemera or *Ephemeroptera* is the name given to natural upright winged insects. Mayfly and olives are the most common of this class the most important of which are *Ephemera Danica* and *Ephemera Vulgata* (Mayflies). Also belonging to this class are the Iron Blues, Large Dark Olives, Blue Winged Olive and Pale Wateries. All these insects produce high density short lived (ephemeral) hatches which can drive the trout into a feeding frenzy, guaranteed to set fishermen's pulses racing!

Eutrophication

A eutrophic water is a highly rich fertile one usually alkaline in nature. As long as the balance of nutrients is kept in check, the trout fare extremely well in eutrophic waters. Eutrophication is not a welcome development however for it means over enrichment which can lead to deoxygenation of the water and eventual fish death. Overly abundant algae blooms are a feature of eutrophication which is usually but not always caused by over zealous application of fertilisers on surrounding agriculture. The leakage of phosphates and nitrates into water can cause unwelcome over enrichment. Where a water is acid in nature their introduction may actually help fertility but where the water is already rich, eutrophication is the result.

Evening Fishing
Great play is often made of fishing during the evening when the bright sun of the day has gone off the water. Undoubtedly it's a time when stubborn trout can come on the rise. Equally your intentions can become less obvious as the shadows lengthen. It's a special time when the silence of night begins to fall and the only noise may be the slurp of a trout gulping down a fly. Evening fishing is tremendously aesthetic and good for the soul but can be a frustrating business if the hatch is short lived. Anglers look for a fall of *spinners* or spent flies but if the air suddenly cools this may be over in a flash. You need a dreamy, warm, extended period to make the most of evening fishing.

Eyesight in Trout
The eyes of a trout are critical to its survival as all trout detect their prey

Evening fishing on the Reay Lochs, Caithness, Scotland.

by its movement. If a fish cannot see its food supply it's a goner. A trout's eyes are on either side of its head and are without eyelids. This means it sees images in a different way to humans and also that it is easily blinded in bright light. The trout has two ranges of vision one binocular above his head and one monocular around his body. When attempting to catch trout with a dry fly you are aiming to put the fly but not your shadow on the water surface in the trout's upper field of vision known as the 'window'. This invisible window is above the trout's head fanning out at roughly 45 degrees either side. This makes accuracy with dry fly fishing a little more taxing for us as the trout is using his more limited binocular vision to see the fly. However if we use wet fly down below the water surface in the trout's much wider monocular field of vision (almost 360 degrees) the fish has a greater chance of seeing it. He may not be any more inclined to take it but at least he can sight it better! The amount of light on the water causes the quality of a trout's vision to alter. Trout cannot see as well in brilliant sunshine or at significant depth as the diffuse light diminishes. The fish's eyes do detect different colours of flies however this is tempered by the depth they are viewed. The deeper the fly is fished at the more it assumes a monochrome appearance.

Fancy Flies

In the UK the old term fancy flies meant brightly coloured non specific representations designed purely to stimulate *aggression* in trout. The term has all but died out now but appears to have emanated from making trout flies in similar colourful design to those used for salmon and/or sea trout principally on Scottish and/or Irish lochs. For example the *Dunkeld* was a classic fancy fly as was the *Butcher*.

Feeding

The quality of feeding available for trout in any given water is dependant on the quality of water. Where the water is rich and *alkaline* in nature the range of aquatic insects and invertebrates will be that much great than when a water is *acid*. Trout consume a wide variety of food according to what is most abundant locally. Insects both aquatic and terrestrial, molluscs, smaller fish, crustaceans, beetles, worms and a variety of other aquatic dwelling food sources are consumed. Small vertebrates like *frogs* can be also consumed in fact just about anything a trout can get its jaws around will be happily munched on. The amount of feeding available will vary according to the seasons with Summer being the most abundant time and Winter being the least productive.

Feeding Fish

The time a trout is actively feeding is the time you are most likely to catch him. See also *Working*. Trout in the stream assume their *stations* and feed on morsels brought down to them on the current. Sometimes you are able to spot feeding fish by their rise forms sometimes they are hidden and taking under the surface. It's a similar situation in stillwaters where feeding fish await aquatic and wind-blown hatches as well as consuming available bottom-feeding such as caddis and shrimp. Whether it is still or flowing water a certain degree of travelling by the trout may be involved especially when a rich new food source first makes its appearance on the water. On stillwaters feeding fish are known to travel up wind lanes gulping down newly emerged insects as they go. On rivers some trout show a tendency to *migrate* at certain times of the year to more abundant feeding grounds.

Felt Soles (Waders)

When manufacturers first started using felt on the soles of wading boots there were all sorts of extravagant claims as to their superiority over rubber soles. In actual fact they are both about the same regarding gripping on algae-covered rocks – pretty poor. The only way to be truly safe is to add studs to the felt (or rubber) and these stop the slip immediately. Felt soles are also an embarrassment on wet grass, they slip so much you may spend more time on your backside than fishing. Felt is useful in its lightness but beware of excessive claims as to its non slip qualities.

Ferox Trout

The UK's deeper lakes and lochs hold a fair population of ferox trout. These are large fish which have taken to a high protein piscivorous diet, usually of *charr* but any small fish including other trout is quite acceptable. Ferox are deepwater dwellers and keep a much lower profile than normal brown trout populations. Anglers can catch ferox on the fly but this is rare and probably only occurs when an angler intercepts the big trout's feeding cycle. Ferox are usually found around 40ft down in large stillwaters and the principal method of fishing for them is *trolling* either spinners or dead bait from a boat. Heavy tackle is used as these fish can reach large proportions. Ferox trout over 30lb have been caught in the UK with a 10lb plus fish being taken as an average weight for a ferox. Because they are such avid consumers of other fish ferox sometimes are dismissed as lanky toothy *cannibal* fish. Only elderly ferox show these traits as they are going back and losing condition with the passage of years. Ferox in full bloom are stunningly proportioned trout with deep gold and bronze flanks. They also grow at a fantastic rate, up to three hundred per cent body weight increase in three or four years

Jane Clarke with a magnificent Ferox from Loch Calder, Caithness, Scotland.

is not an uncommon statistic for these immensely strong but beautiful trout.

Fingering

Piano or guitar players know this term as the placement of fingers on particular musical notes. There is a fishing connotation to it however as at one time some anglers used this as a delicate one-handed retrieve rather like the figure of eight only allowing the line to fall at their feet. The difficulty with this form of retrieve was a complete lack of control if a fish took suddenly as there was no natural brake with the *free hand*. It is not much used today and is one of those things that was high on the aesthetic but low on practical appeal.

Fingerling Trout

Small trout no bigger than a finger are *parr* trout which have not yet made it to adulthood. Usually they are between one and two years old. They tend to occupy *stations* in the stream which are less productive in terms of food and more stressful in terms of the force of the current. Fingerling trout in lakes occupy similarly tough habitats. Those who survive this stage of natural selection make good brood stock for the future. Some trout appear to be fingerlings but closer examination reveals a fish which has not been able to grow much past this size because of the harshness of its environment. Disproportionately large eyes are a tell-tail sign in these disadvantaged fish.

Finning Fish

Rainbow trout show a peculiar tendency to waggle their dorsal fins when feeding in calm water. The fish are obviously enjoying a bounty of nymphs or shrimps beneath the water surface and arching their backs to take in the most nourishment. Brown trout also practise finning when focusing on emerging *chironomids*. Sometimes in late evening cruising trout will fin the surface leaving a big V wake as they travel languidly in search of that last morsel before sundown. Basically whenever you see a trout's fin disturb the surface you should be on your mettle for more often than not a finning fish is a taking fish.

Finnock

Finnock (or phinnock) is a UK term given to young sea trout which have not yet spawned. Finnock are normally around a pound in weight and are beautiful silver athletic fish fresh from better feeding at sea. They are mainly caught in an estuary/river mouth environment when they come in as shoals on the tide to *nose* their native river. A high tide coupled with high water in the main river allows the finnock to run quite far inland but they are not capable of spawning at this age. Finnock are supreme fighters

Finnock, the young sea trout.

dashing at the fly and hitting it with a force which belies their size. Normally it is better to return these trout to allow them to grow on to adulthood when they will achieve weights of 5lb to 15lb or so depending on genetically inherited growth rates.

Fins

The fins of a trout provide balance and propulsion, the tail fin being the largest and most powerful. Wild, naturally spawning trout nearly always have beautifully proportioned fins while stocked trout artificially reared in tanks can suffer damaged, worn or broken fins. Some strains of trout show a prominent white edge to their dorsal fins especially at spawning time. It is assumed that this is a 'come hither' signal to other potential mates. This white edging fades in some strains while in others this fin marking remains all year akin to the markings on *Arctic charr*.

Fish Farming

Both in the UK and parts of the US, fish farming activities have been a hugely unwelcome source of controversy. Waste from these farms (in some cases battery factories would be a more appropriate description) can cause detrimental sea bed pollution which takes years to put right. Chemicals used to treat farmed fish have been found to be carcinogenic and parasite infection, notably sea lice, from the farmed fish packed so tightly into the fish cages can spread to migratory wild fish such as sea trout. The inherent problem has been the siting of fish farms in close coastal waters in the path of migratory journeying fish like salmon and trout. Equally the industry in the UK anyway has been poorly regulated, some would say deliberately so in order to safeguard jobs. Successive British/Scottish administrations have shied clear of any hard legislation preferring to support the ideals of hard and fast commercial industry rather than the more ephemeral long term interests wild fish conservation.

Flash

Many anglers like to add a dash of flash to the construction of a trout fly believing that it will increase its fish attraction qualities. If you examine closely the hatching of any insect particularly sedges and olives it quickly becomes clear they do so in a bubble of light (air) which does indeed flash as they split and finally emerge as an upright or roof-winged insect. One of the reasons flash is added to artificial flies is to mimic this phenomenon. This can be done by the addition of tinsel (gold or silver being the most popular tones) or by filmy transparent strips of soft plastic or by glittery twists of material with a special metallic sheen.

Flavilinea

Flavilinea, sometimes colloquially known as 'Flavs', are mayflies (UK olives) common to parts of the USA and Canada notably British Columbia and the Western States. Somewhat confusingly this insect is also known as the Little Western Green Drake or a variety of Blue Winged Olive. John Gierach recommends a Flavilinea Parachute as a good quality imitation. The dressing for this involves a body of dubbed pale olive rabbit fur, wing medium blue dun or white turkey tied in a T base post, Thorax of dubbed pale olive rabbit, parachute hackle of medium blue dun, rib of brown floss and tail of black moose hair cocked slightly forward. This dressing is not dissimilar to a *Sulphur*.

Flexible Fishing

It may seem like stating the obvious to claim that the most successful fishers show the most flexibility while fishing but it is true. You would be surprised how many of us get stuck in one particular mode and hesitate to switch to something different even when it is glaringly obvious current tactics are not working. Flexible fishing means going with what the conditions dictate and reacting accordingly. It can mean changing from dry fly to wet from traditional nymph to bugs or from a floater to a sinking line. The secret is to swap over quickly rather than flog the proverbial dead horse for so long the concentration falls apart.

Flies

Artificial flies have been around for aeons. The earliest record of a (wet) fly dressing goes back to Roman times. In the third century AD a Roman named Aelian wrote of using a fly made of red wool and cock feathers to try and catch the 'spotted fishes' in his local river. *Wet flies* are still constructed from wool, fur, tinsel and feather though of course today we follow fashion with a variety of new materials notably those which provide the fly with a *flash*. Modern wet fly design falls into three main categories, those made with the plain traditional swept back wing, those made with hackles sometimes colloquially known as *wingless wonders* and then there are *nymphs*. By comparison the *dry fly* is a

Flies.

newcomer to the trout scene. It was not until the latter half of the nineteenth century that the floating dry fly took off. Though he did not single handedly invent it, F M Halford's name is synonymous with the popular use of dry fly on English rivers. By the end of the nineteenth century it was widely thought that the only fashionable way to catch an English trout was by fishing a dry fly upstream. This belief created a lot of unwanted snobbery around river fishing and the *purist* cult was born.

Float Tubes

Also known as belly boats in the USA, these rubber ring or U-boat shaped float tubes have been around in the UK since the early 1990s. This is an exciting way of fishing which really puts you in touch with your environment. Trappings for using a float tube include neoprene and flippers as well as your usual rod and line. Once suitably attired you step into your float tube, strap yourself to the interior seat, back into the water, sit down and paddle off. The wind pushes you along in a sort of a mini *drift* and you simply cast as you go. Once you've finished at your chosen spot you simply lean back and flip your flippers until you have returned to the starting point. Advantages of a float tube over a boat are the much lower centre of gravity which puts you very near the trout without scaring them. To a trout a float tube and its occupant must look like an oversized duck in the water. It is also much more eco friendly (your legs are the engine) and has a very intimate feel to it. Disadvantages are that it is tremendously hard work on the leg muscles. In a strong wind you have to paddle your flippers like mad to get anywhere. Also on a busy boat water you run the risk of being run down. Despite these threats float tubing has its dedicated band of followers throughout the States and the UK.

Floating Line

A fly line which floats is the most popular for low water and/or small stream work as well as being the definitive accessory for successful *top of the water* fishing. Once we got past the era of horsehair and silk lines the plastic coated floating line followed on. The initial concept was simple; coat a thread line with soft supple plastic to make it float on the surface of the water. However first attempts at this were brutally brittle rather like casting a barbed wire twist however as manufacturing techniques took off the modern-day floating line took shape. Coating the finished fly line with all sorts of secret recipe silicones makes the fly line slip through the rings faster. This harps back to the days of 'greased line' salmon fishing first referred to in the early twentieth century when salmon were tempted on small flies and a greased (floating) line.

Fluorescent Materials

Fluorescent materials are added to the composition of a fly to make it glow underwater. The true effectiveness of this depends on the clarity of water and how deep the fly is fished. A wide range of materials is available including chenille, holographic tubing, micro fibres, Krystal Flash and many others. See also *Flash*.

Fluorocarbon

Fluorocarbon is a material akin to nylon used to make the *leader*. Manufacturers claim that fluorocarbon sinks faster than nylon, has more abrasion resistance and has higher knot strength. Whether you believe their assertions is your own decision but do bear in mind the fact that most leader material is of good quality these days and that lost trout are normally caused from anglers not checking their leader for wind knots and abrasions and/or tying the fly on poorly so that the knot slips and the fish is lost.

Fly Box

The design of fly boxes has evolved through generations. Some of the earliest boxes were not boxes at all but parchment sheaves put together like a little book circa 1600s. Later followed round flat tins or leather and sheepskin-lined wallets into which the angler put the gut *cast* with fly or flies attached. It was important the cast did not dry out as it would become brittle and break therefore the flat tins would have a lining of wool or similar which could be kept wet with water or stained with tea. Storing the fly in this manner did not do the hackles any favours and when dry fly came on the scene, special little sectioned boxes with clear pop-up compartments appeared on the market. Wooden boxes were also used to store flies often being given as presentation gifts as it is difficult for the roving angler to carry heavy wooden boxes around while fishing. Today aluminium or plastic boxes with foam are probably the most practical and popular. When buying a plain lined box make sure there is enough space between lid and interior to allow the hackles of flies to stand up properly otherwise you end up with a lot of squashed patterns.

Fly Tying

In the earliest days of angling flies were nearly always tied 'in hand'. *Vices* had not been invented. This meant some pretty dextrous fingers had to be employed in order to catch in wings, body and hackles as appropriate. *Hooks* had to be hand held while materials were wound about them. If you try this today you will find it an immensely difficult task even for the most nimble amongst us. Earliest descriptions of the way to physically tie a fly are found in writings from the 1600s. Unfortunately the *Treatise* of the

1400s only described dressings of flies not how to tie them. From those early techniques of reverse winged flies (a now almost defunct method of tying the wings in the wrong way) a wide variety of skills emerged including how to make split winged or roll winged flies and methods of applying hackles, dubbing in bodies of fur or wool, and making detached body mayflies all followed on. Today fly tying is big business with many companies specialising in supplying the plethora of materials needed to make that perfect fly.

Food Chains
In nature all creatures need a chain of sustenance to exist. Trout are no different in this and a typical circular chain would be algae ~ smaller invertebrates ~ larger invertebrates and small fish fry ~ trout ~ bigger fish e.g. pike ~ fish-eating birds excrete back into water ~ algae ~ invertebrates and so on (~eaten by). If part of this chain is disrupted for example by a severe winter decreasing algae production the evolution of the whole chain can be slowed. A severe pollution incident wipes out the entire chain leading to a complete loss of habitat for all until the water recovers which can be several years down the line. Anglers will sometimes underestimate the importance of these cycles expecting everything in the wild on a plate, sadly it doesn't happen that way.

Foul Hook
If you impale your hook in a trout anywhere except the mouth/lip area you have foul hooked it. Foul hooking can occur when a trout has seen your fly but turned away as you are retrieving it only to have the hook snag its fin or flank. Foul hooked fish do not play in the same way as a normal catch and feel heavy and awkward on the end of your line. Some fisheries demand a foul hooked fish should be returned as it is not seen as sporting. This is fair comment however if the trout is bleeding badly when eventually landed it is kinder to kill it as the wound is likely to become infected and the trout will die a lingering and unpleasant death.

Free Hand
The free hand is the hand not engaged in holding the rod. Many novice anglers do not appreciate the importance of this hand as it helps maintain *balance* in casting and controls the speed at which the line is released on the forward cast. When I am assisting beginners I always emphasise the free hand as the controlling hand.

Freestone
This terms originated from the US where rivers with stone and gravel beds

A freestone river.

are often called freestone rivers. That is not to say some rivers in the UK also have similar habitats it is just that the term is principally an American one. Sometimes you will hear anglers talk of 'freestoning' which simply means going fishing on this type of river.

Frogs

Trout being the opportunistic feeders they are will sometimes consume other vertebrates when these are in a vulnerable state. This occurs during frog spawning time in the UK (April) when hundreds of frogs cluster in the shallows of lakes and lochs in order to reproduce. Smart trout quickly latch on to the frogs' exposure and consume the hapless amphibians often when they are locked in the throes of passion. Such a large piece of easily caught protein is not to be ignored especially if the preceding winter has been a lean one. The only limiting factor in this is the size of the trout in comparison to its prey nevertheless stomach autopsies reveal that trout of just over a pound can happily get their jaws round a small frog or two.

Frosts

Fry and frosts don't mix. A sudden frost in early Spring can annihilate vulnerable tiny trout *fry* as they linger in their natal stream. Not only is the extreme cold a hazard, the drying out effect of the frost means water flow can be decreased again leading to small fish mortality. Traditionally in the UK, trout fry will not develop from the fertilised eggs laid down in October/November until the following March and April. This is nature's way of avoiding disaster however because of the fickleness of the weather late frosts can still occur up until June placing the new arrivals under severe threat. The trout compensate for this by depositing thousands of eggs on the *redds* rather than only a small clutch.

Fry

Once a developing trout has gone from egg to alevin the next stage is the fry. Once the perfectly formed trout fry is over an inch long it will begin to feed on midge larvae or similar and take up a territorial position in shallow water. Though they look like they are in a friendly shoal there is no love lost between the fry as they compete for food sources, and it is definitely survival of the fittest. Big mortalities occur during the fry stage. It is estimated that from 750 fry only twenty yearlings will survive (Frost and Brown) and of these you may only get five mature trout over three years of age. Where the trout are of stillwater origin they will often stay in their natal spawning stream for a year or more before dropping back into the main lake. In the fry stage the tiny fish will feed mainly on aquatic insect larvae like midge and caddis but they also consume shrimps and

Frosts can place trout fry under threat.

beetle larvae if these are available. Growth rate of trout depends on the amount of food the fry can consume without undue stress from competition. Climate also plays a significant role in mortalities, see also *frosts*.

Frying Pan Hackle

This is an almost exclusively American term used in describing flies with a big head hackle and bold upright wings. The origin is unknown but presumably it is to do with the shape of the final fly. Various patterns tied thus include the Frying Pan Green Drake and the Frying Pan Pale Morning Dun and these are used to imitate various flies of the olive and mayfly families.

Gadger

This is an exclusively Scottish term for the big bottom-crawling nymphs of the stonefly. Under the microscope they look all the world like tiny scorpions and they are indeed a voracious feeder on other smaller nymphs and larvae. They are big enough to attach to a small size hook and can be fished as bait where local rules allow. Particularly popular on the River Clyde near Glasgow especially in the early half of the season when they are fished on a fly rod.

Garden Fly

When the conditions for fly fishing are so tough as to be not true, anglers will sometimes indulge in a little lateral thinking and come up with a garden fly. This is usually a worm bait dug up fresh from their garden that morning. On some waters this practice will be viewed as illegal however there are times when *gillies* will slip on a garden fly especially if their guest has been struggling over a lengthy period to catch a fish. Not quite as effective for trout as for salmon but still an old poachers' trick to be reckoned with.

Generic Flies

All flies are descended from a generic few which can be given as winged flies, head hackled flies, palmered hackle flies and nymphs without any hackle or wing. The original winged flies recorded in the *Treatise* in the 1400s were all wet versions fished sunk or at least fished as they fell. Later versions from the nineteenth century onward distinguished between wet and dry fly wing designs, the latter always has its wings prominently standing up from the body.

Genes

The importance of maintaining genetic integrity in a trout population should never be underestimated. Native trout born in the same habitat for several generations without any different stock being introduced develop survival genes unique to their particular water. These genes determine the fishes' particular patterns of *behaviour* including when and where they reproduce and how they will interact with their brethren. Various studies have been carried out worldwide to show how even within one lake or river system separate races of trout can co-exist. In the UK a significant study on Lough Melvin in Ireland showed three distinct populations of trout (*Gillaroo, Sonaghen* and *Ferox*) all residing and spawning as separate entities within this big stillwater. Restocking practices in the UK from the late 1800s saw many unique trout populations genetically corrupted when the stocked fish went on to breed with the native residents. Some populations of trout still exist with their genetic line virtually intact from the last Ice Age colonisation but these are usually found only in isolated waters where restocking practices have not been carried out.

Ghost Tip

This refers to a fly line with a clear intermediate tip fused on to a full floating line. This allows the fly to fish deeper while still letting the angler lift off and cast again relatively easily. Ghost tips are often used in competition angling when the trout are known to be lying a few feet down but not so far as to need the full *sinking line*. See also *Sink Tip*.

Gila Trout

The iridescent gold Gila trout is a native of New Mexico and the White Mountains of Arizona. It is typically more golden in colour than the *Apache trout* and is more genetically associated with rainbow trout. Though the species are classified as 'threatened' in the US the Gila trout still inhabits some of the small headwater creeks and rivers of the south-west. Hybridisation with other trout notably rainbows and a general loss of good habitat places the Gila in a precarious position however local initiatives in keeping the strain genetically intact are underway.

Gillaroo

The Gillaroo is a beautiful Irish trout with a distinctive red spotted hue. It is specific to Lough Melvin but over the years experiments with transporting Gillaroo to other lochs notably in Scotland have been tried with varying degrees of success. The name Gillaroo is an English corruption of the Gaelic *gillie rudh* meaning red boy or fellow. Apart from their high density red spots the Gillaroo can be recognised by their thickened stomach walls which they have developed in order to help deal with the high proportion of snails and crustaceans they consume. Their flesh is also bright red and the trout makes delicious eating.

Gillie

The Scottish gillie (sometimes spelt ghillie) came to prominence during the 1800s when it became fashionable to take to the highlands for sport accompanied by your servant helper or gillie. The gillie was expected not only to be the general dogsbody carting all the gear and/or rowing the boat, but also to be a reasonable angler himself well able to put his client over the best trout or salmon lies. In the early 1900s it was common for highland estates to employ a raft of knowledgeable gillies who were expected to be on call for all manner of angling tasks. Today only the grandest of estates still maintain a gillie service and even then it will usually be to assist in salmon rather than trout fishing. The term gillie (pronounced geelee) is derived from the Gaelic word *gille* meaning young boy.

Gills

Checking under the gill covers of a trout will always give a good indication of its state of health. The interior gills should be bright red in colour indicating a good oxygen absorption rate. If they are grey or brown or have parasites present, the fish is not in prime condition. It could be that it is a very old fish going back or suffering from parasite infestation or there may be a detrimental change in water quality. Over-enrichment of waters can sometimes cause problems in the gills of trout and with serious eutrophication, fish mortality will occur.

Glitter

In bright sunshine the leader is often prone to glitter especially if it has not been given a matt finish. In very clear water, glitter can be a problem but it can be partly solved by using a coloured nylon though remember brown nylon looks like an odd black line to a trout beneath the surface. Top anglers prefer to use clear nylon with a non-shiny surface. If you have clear nylon and wish to make it matt then a glob of earth (clay is particularly good) rubbed along the offending glittery bit does the trick.

Globugs

Globugs look like salmon eggs on a hook and indeed they are often fished as such. Favourite colours are orange, red or a dusky pink. Making them yourself can be tricky as the more you wind on fluorescent chenille or similar the more uneven the circular ball looks. The lazy or less determined among us will buy them from a shop. To fish them properly they need to be well sunk and trundled along in the current to look like an escapee egg tumbling off the redds. Trout take them hard and confidently showing they are opportunistic feeders especially in the Spring after a hard Winter.

Golden Olive Bumble
The flies of the *Bumble* series have already been covered however this particular version is worthy of a mention all of its own. Few stillwater flies in the UK beat this pattern for its trout-attracting qualities especially when mayfly or cow dung fly are on the water or the trout are busy on freshwater shrimp. Quite simply it looks like a sensational mouthful for a trout. The dressing should be straggly and a deep gold colour. It is basically an Invicta without a wing with a yellow gold seal's fur body, gold rib, palmered yellow hackle and blue jay head hackle.

Golden Trout
Golden trout are a rare type of fish found in parts of California and Mexico. The golden trout of California are an exquisite orange gold with a heavily spotted tail with few spots along the flanks while the Mexican trout have prominent parr markings and a rose hue along their flanks. There are golden trout populations also present in Scotland and Switzerland though the status of these teeters on the brink of extinction. These golden trout have different colours from their American counterparts with heavily black spotted backs and flanks and a dark burnished gold hue. All of these unique trout are under considerable threat from loss of habitat and/or hybridisation with introduced fish like rainbows.

Goldheads
The addition of a weighted gold coloured head to a lure became popular in the UK during the 1970s when rainbow trout reservoir fishing suddenly took a dramatic growth spurt. Adding the goldhead meant an extra sunk fly to reach those deeper lying fish. Gold heads were the original design of weighted fly, today we have bead heads, golden nuggets and golden bullets but they basically do the same thing. Typical patterns would be the Goldhead Montana and the Goldhead Cat's Whisker neither of which make any pretext at *purism*.

Grasshopper
In the US the grasshopper is a popular fly particularly well used on the waters of the Western States. It is one fly pattern which has no real UK equivalent there being no natural grasshopper feeding for British trout. The pattern looks like a Large Red *sedge* crossed with a leggy *Hopper* then topped off with a clipped deerhair head. Though it may look a bit

incongruous to the *purist* on windy days with a big wave there seems no reason why it should not bring up a few rainbows or browns in those larger UK stillwaters.

Gravel

Clean gravel free of silt and mud is one of the first prerequisites of good trout habitat. The gravel should be about the size of a reasonably plump grape with some smaller pea-sized gravel mixed in. The gravel is necessary for good spawning habitat as it is this that acts as a little nest for the laid down trout eggs and protects them over the winter. Gravel beds in rivers and lakes also provide good wading though beware in flash floods which make the gravel erode and disappear beneath your feet. In lakes where there is no access to a spawning stream available trout have been known to construct redds on a gravel shore which is well oxygenated by wave action. This is not the best of natural spawning habitat as these shores often dry out once Summer arrives but nevertheless it is better than nothing.

Gravid

If you catch a female trout close to spawning time she will be full of eggs and is said to be gravid. Any gravid fish caught in a water where stocks of wild fish are at a low level should be immediately gently returned. The lady carries the future generations and she deserves your utmost care and respect.

Grayling

Trout anglers in Britain and select parts of Europe notably the Scandinavian countries can enjoy fishing for grayling along with catching trout. Though they have a trout-like shape and are reasonably athletic, in the UK they are classed as a coarse fish with a different open and close season to the trout. Grayling may be fished for over the Winter months when trout are off limits and they can provide welcome sport in reasonable conditions. They are instantly recognisable with their extra large dorsal fin and grey shining flanks with only a few small black spots present. In parts of Europe they are considered an eating delicacy though in the UK trout and salmon are still the most popular in the culinary stakes. Grayling are almost exclusively a flowing water shoaling fish and spawn in late April and May when anglers are concentrating on game fish. In this way they do not pose any significant threat to trout populations in the same habitat.

Green Midge

The Green Midge (large and small) is a predominantly summer hatching *chironomid* found on lakes and rivers throughout the UK. The Large Green Midge is a handsome fellow for an insect bearing more than a passing resemblance to a big green mosquito, trout really go for these if there is nothing much else on the menu. Effective imitations include the Greenwell's Glory the Green Priest and the Olive Bumble.

Green Peter

This is a highly practical Irish fly principally for use on stillwaters. It has sedge and midge connotations and is useful as a top dropper on *loch style* tackle. The fly should have a nice straggly appearance and to this end the body of green seal's fur or substitute should be well picked out. The rest of the fly has a gold tinsel rib, speckled grey pheasant wing and ginger hen hackle at the head. Flies with a hint of green like this one often work when the traditional blacks and browns are failing.

Greenback Trout

The Greenback trout is a sub species of the American *cutthroat*. It is native principally to the South Platte and Arkansas River and is distinguished from its other brethren by its unusually large black spots clustered near the tail of the trout. Red flashes on the gill cover also distinguish this uniquely beautiful trout which is very similar to the Colorado River Cutthroat.

Greenwell's Glory

One of the most famous traditional flies of the UK, the Greenwell's Glory was invented in the mid 1800s by James Wright of Sprouston, Roxburgh. Wright tied the fly for keen angler Canon Greenwell hence its final name. The Canon had spotted a particular insect of olive character on the River Tweed in Scotland and asked a local fly tyer of the period to make a copy. Since then the dressing has not changed that much for the wet fly with a body of waxed yellow tying silk, rib gold thread, wing starling and hackle of *Coch Y Bondhu* hen. Dry Greenwell's and the Greenwell Nymph were later additions to the repertoire and these are particularly useful for hard and bright conditions. Few flies surpass the Greenwell's for imitating olives on both river and stillwater and its still found in the majority of fly boxes over 150 years later.

Grip

Beginners tend to grip the cork on their rod handle so tightly their knuckles turn white. To ensure relaxed, easy casting, a light grip is essential. After all you are putting a fly weighing but a few micrograms upon the water not a lead brick. Grip should only be firm when lifting line off the water and then again when you physically put the line out. Check

To ensure relaxed casting a light grip is essential.

out the best casters at game fairs, you will see they relax when the line is in the air and use the rod as a lever rather than a hammer. Too tight a grip leads to clumsy awkward technique, keep it soft to avoid tension and painful tennis elbow!

Grouse Wing Flies

Grouse winged flies form a stable of old traditional UK patterns still in use throughout the UK. Some say the fly may have originated in Ireland rather than Scotland but wherever they first came from, grouse wing flies are invaluable for imitating any winged insect including olives and sedges. Among the most popular tyings are the Grouse and Claret, Grouse and Green, Grouse and Purple and Grouse and Yellow. All these patterns feature a tail of GP tippets, wool or seal's fur body according to colour choice, black head hackle and the grouse wing. Mallard is sometimes substituted for the grouse wing and this is perfectly acceptable. These flies are fished wet as part of a *loch style* team and can represent either the nymph or the hatched insect.

Growth of Trout

How fast a trout will grow in a particular water is down to its genetic make up, then availability of food and the amount of competition present. *Genes* can determine the overall size to which a trout can grow for optimum survival however if a small 8in stream trout is displaced into a eutrophic fertile lake the trout will grow in size despite its genetic makeup. Trout in rich environments with a wide selection of food have the potential to grow much quicker than trout in harsh *acidic* waters. If the *competition* for food is intense either amongst fish of the same species or from different types then the stress of this may inhibit the overall growth of the trout. Some factors which determine the final size of trout i.e. those fish anglers most want to catch, include the specific growth rate seen in their first year of life as this varies considerably amongst different trout populations. Also the age at which the trout first matures and spawns and the overall length of adult life before the fish dies. In the UK *Leven* trout have been known for centuries as fast growing trout spawning at around the age of four and then dying at about seven years of age. This contrasts well with the *Ferox* which grows very slowly in the first few years of life then suddenly accelerates at around the age of three years doubling or trebling its weight in a year or two and then living to a ripe old age of fifteen years plus.

Gut

Earliest anglers knew no such niceties as *fluorocarbon, poly leaders* or *nylon*. After the good old horsehair twisted down to a single strand 'leader', the next invention was a silk line with a gut leader on to which the fly was attached. In the mid 1800s gut was made from the entrails of a silk worm before it had shed its silk though later sheep's intestines provided a reasonable substitute to this hard to obtain material. It is interesting that the gut was effectively tapered like the horsehair. W C Stewart circa 1850 described a length of triple gut attached to the 'winch line' at one end and then a length of 'picked gut' at the other to which the fly was attached. Gut was notorious for breaking if it became at all dry hence it had to be kept damp and soaked in cold water before use. It also glittered like crazy in any bright sunshine and had to be stained with copperas or cold tea. Altogether the invention of nylon was a welcome relief as gut was hard work!

Habitat

A good trout habitat is one which provides clean well oxygenated water, a wide and plentiful range of food and a degree of shelter both from predators and the elements. Adequate spawning facilities with good *gravel* present are also necessities in a user-friendly trout environment. Habitat degradation occurs when the water becomes polluted in some way either in the main watercourse and/or in side spawning streams. Pollution incidents are the most common cause of a loss of invertebrate feeding for the trout (see also *Food Chains*). Loss of habitat also occurs when shelter from bankside vegetation (grasses, bushes and trees) is cut down or overgrazed by livestock. Dams also cause unnatural water height fluctuations leading to both a loss of natural feeding as well as loss of access to spawning environment. *Climate change* can also lead to spawning areas drying out and consequent loss of habitat.

Hackle

Mention of using a hackle (or its earlier spelling hakyll) in the making of a fly first comes around the time of the *Treatise* circa 1400s. Usually the feathers used for making a hackle come from the neck of a particular bird rather than its wings. Hackles may be *palmered* or used only at the head of the fly or as throat hackle. They may be tied in very sparse as in the Stewart *Spider* range or can be bushy and overlaid as in *dapping flies*. The addition of a hackle was probably first done with the intention of giving the fly more lifelike appearance. Soft hackles used in wet fly fishing will pulse in a very lifelike way beneath the surface while stiff hackles make a dry fly stand up well when it alights upon the water surface.

Hairwing Flies

This term simply means the wing of an artificial fly is made from animal hair (squirrel, bucktail, deer, stoat etc) rather than from birds' feathers. At one time in the UK, hairwing flies were almost exclusively used for salmon fishing. Straggly flies like the Stoat's Tail or the Munro Killer do exceptionally well for sea trout as well as salmon. Today the use of hairwing flies by UK trout anglers is increasing although many fishers remain deeply traditional and tend not make as much use of hairwing flies as they might. The opposite is true in the USA were numerous local trout flies are made in the hairwing genre using elk hair, bucktail or similar. All hairwing trout flies are tied on single hooks rather than the double and treble hooks more common to salmon angling.

Halcyon Days

Every angler past a certain age harks back to the ephemeral 'halcyon days' when big trout rose freely, the air was pure and the stream ran clear. Days when the only other companion you were likely to see was an otter, a heron, a loon or a roebuck (insert your own appropriate native species) and over crowded angling had not yet been born. While there is no doubt as to the sweeping manmade changes to trout habitat being seen worldwide, we ourselves should shoulder some of the blame for those lost halcyon days. While memories can play tricks as to the true size of those trout we so cleverly fooled there is no doubt that greedy over-fishing played its part in creating the changed stock levels of wild trout that we now see across global trout habitats. *Stocking* has long been seen as a way to recreate the good times however loss of indigenous strains of trout are nearly always the result of such actions. Halcyon days indeed.

Hands

When an angler has good 'hands' it simply means he or she controls rod and line well and feels the trout almost before it has taken a proper hold. Sounds a bit like an excuse for someone's superior ability to catch fish however if you want to suss out who is an experienced fisher and who is just starting out, nine times out of ten their hands will give it away. Novices have a certain tension and clumsiness in their hands while seasoned anglers' hands are relaxed and in confident control, see also *Grip*.

Seasoned anglers' hands are relaxed and in control.

Hard Water

Hard (as opposed to soft) water is just another term for an *alkaline* aquatic environment. In general terms the growth rate of trout in hard water is better than in *acid* (soft) water. Any freshwater lying over a chalk and/or limestone habitat is likely to be hard rather than soft in nature.

Hare's Ear

The fur from a hare's ear can be used in the making of the body of a trout fly. Usually it is put on as a *dubbing* and its light brown whiskery appearance gives a fine general representation of legs, feelers, antennae etc. The Gold Ribbed Hare's Ear (GRHE) sometimes known as the Hare Lug is one of the best known nymph patterns for river angling and is also an extremely successful pattern on stillwaters in semi-calm conditions. Hare's ear flies are mainly used as a general representation of olive nymphs or sedge pupae but can also be taken as freshwater shrimps. The original wet version was tied in the 1800s if not earlier and the dry variants came along at the end of the nineteenth century when the cult of dry fly first took hold. Courtney Williams in *A Dictionary of Trout Flies* gives the standard wet fly (nymph) dressing as tying silk – yellow, body – dark hare's ear dubbed, rib – flat gold tinsel, 'hackle' – longer strands of hare's ear picked out with a dubbing needle, whisks – three strands of the head hackle. This is a timeless fly well capable of producing trout anywhere in the UK if not worldwide.

Hatch

'Hatching flies bring on a rise' is a well proven rule of thumb for trout fishers everywhere. A hatch is an emergence of a particular insect usually from nymph/pupae stage to adult flying stage. Hatches can be small in number or can almost carpet a water in their intensity, mayfly being a typically abundant example of this natural phenomenon. Once trout start to feed on the hatch either when first emerging or as a fall of spent flies, they switch into feeding mode and this is normally the time when anglers have the most chance of intercepting a fish. Though our angling ancestors deliberately copied the prevailing natural fly hatch, the term *'matching the hatch'* (trying to exactly represent the insect most prevalent on the water) does not appear to come into angling terminology until the 1900s. Exact equivalents of the hatch are sometimes not necessary when the trout are extremely active, a lot depends on overhead conditions. For example for wild brown trout an exact representation of the hatch is normally required in very clear water with bright sun.

Hatchery

The practice of breeding trout for stocking purposes in hatcheries goes back over many centuries. In the UK trout farming reached a peak from the mid 1800s to the outbreak of the First World War. British reared trout were transported as fertilised eggs from the mid 1800s onward to such far away colonial bases as New Zealand, Argentina, India and South Africa. By the early 1900s many large country estates in Scotland and England had their own hatcheries run by their own game keeping staff. Hatchery-reared brown and rainbow trout have been added to many UK waters in an effort to increase sport from the middle of the nineteenth century. This practice upset the genetic apple cart so much so that many wild brown trout in the UK are in fact descendants of introduced fish which have spawned with the native trout. Introduced rainbow trout have not spawned as successfully in the wild in the UK and only a handful of naturally regenerating populations exist.

Hatchery-Bred Trout
In general terms stocked trout, especially those added into a water system at weights of over a pound, fair far worse than their counterparts born and bred in a specific wild habitat. Hatchery-reared trout of many generations are especially tame and because they are used to taking their food as soon as it hits the tank water surface, they are often the first caught by fishermen in commercial waters. Stocked fish can become highly competitive in tanks and when placed into a freshwater system where wild/native trout also exist they may have a detrimental effect on the indigenous species. This is especially true at spawning time when the introduced fish bully and harry the wild fish off the redds. Given half a chance the brown trout stockies hybridise with the native trout and genetically pure strains can be severely disrupted. However this effect is balanced by evidence suggesting that stocked trout survive less well in the natural environment. See also *Stocked Trout*.

Hats
Head gear in trout fishing is an absolute must. A hat keeps glare and stray flies away from your eyes and no angler should be without this accoutrement. Whether it's a fedora, peaked cap, deerstalker, flaps or a flat cap their importance can never be understated. Just remember and buy hats which suit your local fishing environment i.e. have one which keeps you warm in Winter and a cool one for Summer neither of which should blow off in a gale.

Head of a Trout Fly
Traditionally the head of the trout fly is usually fashioned by whip finishing the tying silk below the eye of the hook and then adding a blob of

varnish to secure it all together. Heads could either be the same colour as the main body of the fly or a different colour of tying silk and/or varnish could be added. The head of the fly plays an important part in securing hackles and wings, if poorly fashioned the fly breaks up after a few sessions. Modern materials allow heads to be made from beads of different weights and hues. This can add shiny glamour to the fly while serving a specific purpose either in fish attraction or taking the fly down to a depth where the trout might be feeding.

Heather Fly

The heather fly (*Bibio pomonae*) is a terrestrial bred insect hatching off heathery moorland in significant numbers during September in the UK, see also *Bibio*. This insect is related to the hawthorn fly and both types are found throughout the British Isles. It has a black body, flat shiny wing and red legs. In some areas the heather fly is also known as 'red legs' or simply 'Bibio' but whatever their name the trout go crazy for them almost as much as any mayfly hatch. The fact that the heather fly is a poor flyer often blown straight on to the water in a good breeze also contributes to its acceptability. Common UK patterns used to imitate the heather fly include the Black Ke He and the Bibio.

Height of Water

Water height can dictate fishing tactics. High water in rivers may require heavier flies and the use of sinking or intermediate lines. Low water normally requires much lighter tackle with floating line and a lighter more delicate range of flies. After considerable rainfall, water height in rivers will rise and the stream may become cloudy for a time. Trout gorge themselves on the extra invertebrate life being swept down on the current however they are harder to catch on the fly owing to poor water clarity. In stillwaters a rise in water height either natural or manmade also brings about extra feeding for the resident trout however a fall in water height can lead to important feeding areas drying out and a loss of *habitat*.

Hippers

Hippers is an exclusively North American term for thigh *waders*. Of particular use when wading is only required to just above the knee in fast flowing waters, deeper wading requires chest waders to avoid annoying splashes creeping over the top of the boots.

Hi Vis Flies

Flies made specifically from high visibility materials are known as hi vis flies in the UK. The idea behind this pattern is to use bright sparkly materials which can be seen underwater from a fair distance off. Of particular use on stillwaters where the water clarity is poor and more commonly used for rainbows rather than browns. Fly lines also sometimes carry this abbreviation, it just means they are easier to see.

Hook a Trout

To hook a trout a *strike* of some sort is usually required. Sometimes the fish simply hits the fly so hard it hooks itself however a more tentative pluck at the line may require a quick action to sink the hook before the trout is off again. The simplest way to hook fish is to feel the trout pull one way and you then pull the other by lifting the rod tip to put tension on the line between you and the fish. A firm tension must be maintained otherwise the trout may come off. When taking the fly the trout will normally be hooked at the side of its mouth in the scissors however the hook may also be lodged on the tongue or lip. Occasionally the fish will have taken the fly so confidently it is almost down the gullet and forceps may be required to remove the hook. When setting the hook it is important to strike smoothly but not overcook it otherwise you can end up almost breaking the jaw of the trout or pulling the fly away before the fish has taken hold.

Hooks

Hooks for fishing have been found to be in use as far back as the sixth century BC. Ancient hooks were fashioned from bone, stone, iron, bronze, wood or shell. Eyed and barbed hooks have also been around since BC despite claims to the contrary by some ill-informed Victorians. Modern hooks are made from a variety of metals specially treated for strength, durability and anti-rust qualities. Eyes can be made 'up' generally for dry fly, or 'down' for wet flies. The shape of the hook can also be fashioned in different curves to accommodate different types of nymph or shrimp patterns. Streamer/lure designs are often found on long shank hooks while more subtle designs are made on the shorter shank. Wide or narrow gape, micro barbed, offset points, sweeping bends and sproat forged are all terms associated with hook design. Hook sizes for trout vary between 8 (large) and 22 (small) with hooks in the 10 to 16 range being the most commonly used.

Hoops

In trout accuracy casting competitions you will normally be asked to get your 'fly' i.e. a bit of red wool inside a series of floating hoops placed as different distances from the bank. Unfortunately the way this is done bears little resemblance to the delicacy needed to attract a wild trout to your fly. The line is slammed up and down as quickly as possible from hoop to hoop in order to gain the most points in a prescribed time. Hoop

Hoppers.

accuracy is a much better description of it as this technique would scare off any self respecting fish!

Hoppers

Hoppers are mini versions of *Daddies* and given the right conditions they are as good at attracting trout. They can be made to fish wet or dry and their most distinct feature is the six knotted legs tied in to the body. Hoppers can be dressed sparse or heavy and come in a variety of shades from amber to black. Claret and Olive Hoppers are also popular. Trout tend to smash into these general patterns and whatever it is they are supposed to be imitating they love them. The only time Hoppers can fail is in semi-calm conditions otherwise look out for heart-stopping takes. A firm favourite amongst UK anglers is the Black Hopper made on size 10 or 12 hooks with black seal's fur body, green or silver tinsel rib, six knotted black pheasant tail fibre legs and a head hackle of black hen tied fairly sparse.

Horsehair Lines

The earliest anglers had to make their own fly lines twisting down horsehair tail strands until a single strand of hair was left on to which they tied the fly. There was no separation of line and leader rather it was all cleverly tapered to a point. Venables circa 1600 describes the most important facet of making a good horsehair line as keeping the twisting of strands even '...to make the line well, handsome, and to twist the hair even and neat, makes the line strong'. He also added 'I do not like the mixing of silk or thread with hair' as he had found that this made the line rot quicker in water. Strands from grey or white horses were considered best, perhaps they were a little stronger than brown or black hair. Today horsehair has gone, however it is nice to think our modern tapered leaders were born out of this ancient craft.

Hump-Backed Trout

In the UK in the late 1800s Victorian pioneers were given to naming trout by their shape and/or colour. The hump-backed trout was one such example being found only in remote lochs in the county of Sutherland in northern Scotland. This type of trout was wrongly described as a separate species rather than a distinct strain. It could have been distantly related to the *Gillaroo* which has thickened stomach walls in order to cope with digesting snails and other crustaceans. Alternatively it may have been subject to disease causing an odd deformity in the fish. Whatever gave this trout its name it's a fish rarely encountered today.

Humpy

The Humpy is a popular American fly of special note. It is rather like a heavily dressed *Wulff* crossed with an overdone *Adams*. Humpys are particularly good at bringing up otherwise quiet fish as they look like a mighty mouthful of insect stuck on the surface. They can be fished as a static dry or in a wave can be retrieved back at sufficient speed to create a wake. Being virtually unsinkable is their only drawback as a more cautious brown trout will try and knock it down and take it below the surface as it would with a natural insect. Of course the Humpy pops straight up again and the fish can miss. Nevertheless this is a top trout taker in the US and is finding more favour in Europe as anglers latch on to its undoubted qualities. The original dressing had a deer hair body, wing and tail and was topped off with a grizzly hackle. Today there are versions incorporating elk hair, moose hair and/or calf tail and you will come across various versions of this fly including the Royal Humpy and the Parachute Humpy.

Ice

When ice forms on freshwater lakes any trout therein seek deeper water preferably near where there is a hidden spring or near an inflowing stream. These features bring in extra oxygen and help the trout survive a frozen aquatic world. When rivers and small streams freeze over the trout will seek the deeper water below the ice and usually prefer a faster *run* nearby to increase their oxygen intake. In very cold temperatures the resident trout in either flowing or stillwater appear to go into a state of torpor. This will save energy reserves during the lean, meanest part of winter. Anglers often experience some difficulty when the ice begins to melt and break up. In rivers ice strands can freeze directly on to the fly line turning it brittle. In Scotland when small ice clumps flow down a stream the resultant annoying mush is called descriptively 'grue'. This hampers your cast and retrieve and disrupts your fishing no end. Lakes have flat mini icebergs for a time but do not seem to suffer the grue plague. See also *Anchor Ice*.

Ice layers form a dramatic pattern on a Scottish loch.

Imitation

If you are using an imitation you are casting a fly which looks more or less like the local hatch. Imitations differ from general representations or attractor patterns as they are supposed to match what the trout is feeding on and stimulate a feeding rather than an aggressive response. In the UK some of the oldest flies mentioned in the *Treatise* are meant as representations of natural insects which implies the art of imitation has been around since time immemorial. See also *Artificial*.

Induce a Take

All anglers are trying to induce a trout to take however it is generally accepted that the late English anglers Frank Sawyer and Oliver Kite took the technique when applied to nymph fishing, one step further. As with all clever concepts it is remarkably simple. When upstream nymph fishing if you employ a light rise and fall of the rod tip as you work the fly in the current, the sunk nymph rises and falls like a natural one. This action is thought to stimulate the waiting fish into feeding and with any luck you will indeed induce a take. That's the theory anyway.

Inspiration

Not strictly a fishing term but nevertheless the greatest inspiration for most anglers is the sight and/or sound of a rising trout. A rise of any sort switches on even the most disheartened of anglers and inspires them to keep trying with one more cast.

Intermediate Line

Apart from the *floating line* the next most popular fly line is usually an intermediate one in the pursuit of trout. The idea here is to fish the fly below the water surface about two or three feet down. Switching to an intermediate is always worthwhile if you are trying to determine the depth the trout are lying as it takes you that bit deeper sinking slowly down without plummeting to the bottom. Intermediate lines are particularly useful in bright conditions where the trout may be laying low and/or in calm conditions when line wake becomes obvious.

Introducing Fish

Restocking on commercial fisheries is usually done by the fish lorry coming along at a set hour and dumping a load of stockies into one spot of the lake or river. These trout take a while to acclimatise and are vulnerable and disorientated. Anglers wanting easy pickings need only to plop a line into the poor bunch and there is a good chance they will pull one of them out. Whether this can be classed as sport is anyone's guess especially if the trout are introduced at a takeable size, *put and take* at its

Introducing trout to a small stillwater.

best perhaps. Introducing trout into a new habitat is often better done when they are fry size, that way they have plenty of time to mark out their own territories and grow at their own pace. The trouble is that some anglers want results right away and fry can take three years or so to become a takeable fish. Striking a balance between good fish management practice and the needs of the customer is never easy.

Invertebrates
Fishermen use the term invertebrates to describe the great melange of bugs with no backbone that trout feed on at various times through the year.

Invicta
The Invicta is a true traditional British wet fly dating from the early 1900s. It was invented by a James Ogden as an imitation of a sedge principally for stillwaters but it is versatile enough for rivers as well. Its secret is its versatility with trout taking it as a small fleeing fish, a shrimp, nymph or an emerging insect. The original dressing was sparsely tied but some modern fly tiers tend to make it more bulky with more hackle. The dressing is simple with yellow seal's fur body, oval gold tinsel rib, palmered red cock hackle, blue jay throat hackle, GP tippet for tail and wing of hen pheasant. Many anglers resort to this fly in difficult conditions especially when a touch of blue is required to attract the trout's attention. The Silver Invicta and the Orange Invicta are excellent variants of the original dressing and equally effective.

Iron Blue
Iron Blues are members of the upright winged family. They are small with dark body and wing with two tails and they hatch on UK rivers mainly in the Spring, April and May are when the hatch is most profuse. When nothing bigger is on the menu, trout will take the Iron Blue with gusto. Good imitations are the Iron Blue Dun, Greenwell's Glory, Willow Fly and Snipe and Purple.

Jackets (Waterproof)
The days of leaky anoraks or ancient battered wax jackets are now virtually gone and given the unpleasant soakings these garments could give us if not properly treated, it is probably just as well. Today we have a wide range of superior materials used in the construction of a fishing

Go for the best waterproof jacket you can afford.

jacket and life is generally more bearable in the rain. If buying a new waterproof go for the best you can sensibly afford. Good quality jackets are made of so called breathable fabric i.e. you don't gather as much sweat inside it as the rain on its exterior. They have well taped and sealed interior seams (the bits that leak in poor quality gear) and are light and soft to wear. Detachable hoods are not as good as they look as the rain can drive in under the join. Go for integral hoods which can be drawn in snug in a gale. Cuffs are also important, they should fit neatly but comfortably at the wrist stopping rainwater entering when you lift your arm to cast. Jackets with pockets are great but remember the more you fill them the more bulky and constrictive the waterproof becomes. Better sometimes to store accoutrements like nylon and flies in a vest and wear the jacket over if it rains.

Jersey Herd

The Jersey Herd was one of the first heavy *lures* made in the UK in the early 1950s. The original was devised by Tom Ivens who gave it the name Jersey Herd after the gold milk bottle top he had used in making its shiny body. The fly imitates swimming small fish or fry and as it sinks like a stone, must be fished deep on a fast retrieve. Today Mylar is often used instead of the metal body however the result is similar. The original dressing was on a longshank hook size 6 to 10 with copper tinsel or lurex, rib copper wire, tail, back and head of peacock herl and head hackle of hot orange hen. Still very effective for stocked rainbows but deeper lying wild trout will take it on occasion.

Jump

On occasion a trout when hooked will jump dramatically to try and shake the hold of the fly. It's a moderately successful tactic if the trout is only lightly attached and most anglers will have witnessed a leap to freedom and felt the consequent sense of loss. Trout which jump naturally without the threat of a nearby angler are doing so for a variety of reasons. They might be leaping to intercept a flying insect or to avoid an unseen predator or competitor which has arrived in their territory. Sometimes they seem to just jump for the heck of it expressing their natural joie de vivre. Wild brown trout have been known to jump two to three feet clear of the water, rainbows show similar acrobatic tendencies. Trout in shallow water appear more acrobatic than those in deep water, who seem to bore down in search of safety when first hooked.

Jungle Cock

Feathers from the jungle cock are highly prized for their apparent oval orange coloured 'eyes' sometimes called cheeks found toward the tip of the feather. These are used for making eyes at the head of *lure* or *streamer* patterns giving the fly a life-like appearance. Brightly coloured salmon flies also often make use of jungle cock in their design.

Kate McLaren

The Kate McLaren is one of those wonderful Scottish dark wingless patterns which while very general in nature can be absolutely deadly in midge and sedge hatches. It works best as a top *dropper* when it is dibbled across the waves before lifting off. It is rather akin to a *Bumble* pattern and its trout attractiveness can be put down to its soft pulsing hackle. It was named after the mother of Charles McLaren a renowned Scottish sea trout angler of the 1960s. The dressing given in McLaren's book the *Art of Sea Trout Fishing* is still the best with GP crest tail, black body (wool or seal's fur), flat silver rib, palmered black hackle with additional head hackle of natural red hen tied over the black. It is excellent on a dull, windy day for sea trout, browns and rainbows.

Keep Net

In the UK keep nets (tunnel nets kept submerged in water) might be associated mainly with coarse fishing however they can also serve a purpose in wild fish management. Trout caught for sampling purposes may be deposited in the keep net without harm until ready for examination and transferral of trout to different waters where permitted, is also assisted.

Ke He

This pattern was first devised in the 1930s by two doctors Messrs Kemp and Heddle fishing on Orkney Isles, Scotland. They made it to represent what they thought was a small bee-like insect (actually the *Bibio* or *Heather Fly*) they had seen hatching off the shore on local lochs. The Ke He was immensely popular during the 1950s to the 1980s and though today it may have been slightly overtaken by other designs it is still an effective pattern for stillwaters everywhere. The dressing is simple with a fairly thick body of peacock herl, GP tippet tail and Rhode island red cock hackle (not palmered). A red wool tail or tag was added to this dressing along the way but can be omitted if wished. The Ke He is not only an effective heather fly imitation, it can also imitate beetles, midge and even at a pinch freshwater shrimp.

Kelts

Kelts are spent fish which have recently spawned and are not recovered back to prime condition. The term is mainly associated with salmon however trout and sea trout can also appear lean with big heads and soft flesh after spawning and are effectively in a kelt condition. In the UK spawned sea trout which have returned to sea may take time to feed up again and if caught in the early season these should by law be returned. The occurrence of brown trout kelts is much rarer as in the UK there is a close season extending from October to March which allows the fish time to recover from spawning. Salmon and sea trout have a far shorter close time which is probably why more kelts are caught with this species.

Kill

Where trout may be killed for the purpose of eating them the easiest way to despatch the fish is by a blow to the head with the aid of a *priest*. Killing fish is also recommended if the trout is bleeding badly from hook penetration. Returning a fish injured in such a way usually leads to an infected wound and may result in a prolonged, uncomfortable death.

Klinkhamer Flies

Originally designed by Dutch fly tier Hans Van Klinken the Klinkhamer was meant to represent an emerging caddis (sedge) fly. The pattern was made on a specially shaped hook which hangs suspended in the surface film. It is distinguished by its buoyant white T shaped *parachute* hackle which holds the head fly just on the surface while its body dangles realistically below. Today the Klinkhamer is used to represent any emerging insect and is highly successful in calm, bright weather. It is tied in a variety of colours with black, brown and green being the most popular.

Knots

Secure knots between fly and leader, leader and fly line and fly line and *backing* are essential. Wind knots however are a downright pain. These unwanted nuisances appear as if by magic in the leader and weaken its strength no end. Fishermen's knots have a variety of names including the Half Blood, Blood Knot, Nail Knot, Turle, Water Knot and the Grinner. One of the most commonly used knots in trout fishing is the Half Blood. To make sure your fly is firmly attached to the leader push the knot down towards the eye of the hook – slipping knots are one of the worst offenders for losing trout.

Kype

The term kype refers to a hooked nose. Male salmon often have

This Ferox has a pronounced kype.

prominent kypes when they are ready to spawn and male trout can show similar characteristics. The kype can act as an aggressive signal to a competitor to keep away from his female mate and may also be a sign of virility to any potential spouse.

Lake Trout

In the UK the lake trout is simply a large brown trout of the *Salmo trutta* family. Colours of UK lake trout vary from deep burnished gold to a dull silvery grey depending on their location, *Ferox* could also be construed as lake trout. However in North America the lake trout is actually a member of the char family preferring deep-cold water habitats. They survive well in nutrient-poor waters and although their growth rate is very slow they can attain a good size, upward of 5lb has been recorded. American lake trout spawn in September and October within the lake rather than

111

running up inflowing streams and favour gravel shorelines where there is a good onshore wind to oxygenate the water. Notable populations are found within Lake Tahoe, Lake Superior and the Great Bear Lake.

Landing Nets

A landing net is essential when boat fishing, preferably one with an extending handle. If competition boat fishing watch your handle length, too long may be deemed cheating! Knotless mesh nets are preferable as it is less damaging to the scales and protective slime of the trout if it is to be returned. Short handled nets are useful when wading far from the shore where a beaching of the trout cannot be easily executed. Go for one with a stretchy cord attachment so you can catch and release your trout easily when wading without struggling to detach the net from your vest. Nets come in a variety of shapes from tear drop to semi triangular, just make sure you have one which is the correct size for the trout you are likely to catch.

Large Dark Olive

The Large Dark Olive is a significant upright winged fly found on a range of UK rivers from alkaline chalkstreams to quite acidic burns. Hatches are at their height through Spring into early Summer and trout rise well to this small but tasty morsel. There are a number of imitations with the Rough Olive one of the most useful. Tie in size 14 and 16 with a sparse dressing. The body is of olive mole, rib fine gold wire, tail of medium olive cock hackle fibres, head hackles of olive and black hen. Some dry versions add a small upright grey wing but in most situations the fly works just as well with or without a wing.

Larvae

Between insect egg and pupa there is a larval stage. Trout like to consume copious amounts of midge and sedge larvae as they are easy pickings especially when there is nothing better hatching on the surface. Red Bloodworm are the larva stage of *chironomids* and these are especially popular with brown trout inhabiting slow moving water. Midge larvae can also be grey or brown in colour and these are just as happily consumed. The larvae of the caddis or sedge fly live on the bottom and make themselves protective cases of grit and plant matter. Most caddis larvae attach themselves to the underside of stones and/or water weeds though some will live in tiny burrows in silt. Trout actively forage for these as they supply additional protein in their diet.

Lateral Line

The lateral line of a trout is that faint line running from head to tail along the fishes' flanks. This provides the trout with an extra sensory organ as it

Landing nets are essential for stillwater fishing.

is full of neuromasts which are highly sensitive to low frequency vibration and local water disturbance. Trout use their lateral line to detect the presence of other fish and predators in their vicinity. It is a kind of hidden third eye to go along with their ears and eyes and warns the trout of anything new entering his or her territory.

Leader

The expression 'leader' has now largely overtaken older terminology like the nylon, cast, gut or similar. The leader (sometimes also known as a tippet) is of course the tool that fills the space between the fly and the fly line. It will be made of nylon, fluorocarbon or monofilament and provides a suitable 'unseen' gap with the intention of fooling the trout into believing your fly is not attached to anything which might do him harm. Leaders have different *Breaking strains* with the most commonly used being between 3 to 6lb BS.

Leven Trout

In Scotland trout which originate from shallow fertile Loch Leven, Kinross are called Leven trout. Trout from Loch Watten in Caithness, closely resemble the strain of trout emanating from Loch Leven probably as their rich shallow aquatic habitats are very similar. They are a particularly beautiful silvery gold athletic fish often with distinctive black asterisk star spots and a few red spots. They can more resemble sea trout and have a migratory roving almost pelagic lifestyle favouring open water habitats. Given that they are a wonderful sporting fish, Leven trout have been used to restock waters across the UK and in such exotic locations as New Zealand, Africa and Patagonia since the 1800s. They are not a particularly long living trout, seven years or so is the norm, and if introduced into an acidic habitat they will quickly lose their silver sheen and revert to the darker gold of the resident fish. Leven trout quite happily breed with other types of brown trout and therefore can quickly lose their original unique characteristics.

Lie(s)

Lies are something that fishermen might tell one another from time to time about the fish that got away however wherever a trout makes his territory can also be described as a 'lie'. The term is often associated with salmon e.g. a good salmon lie but it applies just as much to trout. A good trout lie will be one which offers plenty of easy access to food and good shelter from predators. In rivers the edges of weed beds, behind rocks, pots, small obstructions like fences and the sides of the main run all over trout lies. In lakes anything that breaks up the uniformity of the water for example promontories, reefs, islands, skerries (underwater rocks which just break the surface), edges of weed beds, drop offs etc are all possible trout lies.

Life History (Trout)

Fossil evidence shows us that the family of *Salmoninae* comprising trout, salmon and char were established at least fifty million years ago. *Salmoninae* are themselves part of the *Salmonidae* family comprising of salmon, trout, char, whitefish and grayling. Trout were originally limited to the Northern hemisphere however world-wide *stocking* efforts from the mid nineteenth century onward ensured that trout are now found all around the world. In the UK trout found along the east coast had more migratory tendencies (see *Leven* trout) and were found to be colonisers swimming around the coasts of Britain to mate with the more static strain of west coast trout. Stocking intervention by angling interests meant that the original trout strains were considerably intermingled from the mid 1800s onward. See also *Native Trout*.

Lifejacket

Any angler venturing into deep water either afloat or wading into an unknown fast water river should wear a lifejacket of some sort. This can be the traditional over the head style (which some anglers find too cumbersome to cast with) or a floatation vest. Lifejackets are now made in non-constricting slimline bar form and these are ideal for stillwater fishing. Some lifejackets inflate immediately on impact with cold water, others you have to pull a red tab at the base and this should fire up a little gas cylinder which inflates the jacket. Some floatation vests include all the pockets found in a normal fishing vest and these are popular with the peripatetic angler who enjoys lots of different angling styles and venues.

Lifespan

Different strains of trout show differing length of lifespan. In the UK some deep water trout like the *Ferox* have an average lifespan of fifteen years or so whereas the *Leven* trout seems to lose condition after about seven years and may die not long after this age. Some stream trout may be very small in nature but actually be around a hardy nine years of age, size is often determined by the surrounding habitat. Genetics play a considerable part in determining how long a trout might survive if it is in clean, cool, well oxygenated water, free of any disease and attacks from predators including anglers.

Light (Effects on Trout)

Trout are generally light-sensitive creatures. They have no eyelids and will shy away from bright light shone directly into their eyes. In a river trout

Changes in light intensity will often stimulate trout to feed.

will usually face upstream into the current and if the light is also coming from that direction they may not see the fly as well as when the light is off the water. Similarly in a stillwater, if the wind and light direction are the same the fishing can be more difficult than if they oppose. Trout used to living in bright sunshine and clear water will still rise to the fly but can be more tricky to deceive than trout who enjoy a variable climate and/or a darker stain of water. In general terms fishing in mid Summer when the sun is at its full height is harder work than when fishing early and late in the season when the light comes in at a lower angle and does not penetrate sub surface as much. Light effects are not all bad news however as changes in light will often stimulate trout to feed and the angler should be aware of this as even the slightest variation might mean a change of tactics.

Limestone
Large parts of southern England and some select areas of northern Scotland have limestone present in various forms. These will vary from hard rock rather like granite to soft clay like *marl* with copious chalk beds in between. Most limestone is pale in colour no matter its texture and its presence increases the alkalinity of the water and has a direct bearing on the quality of feeding.

Lined Fish
If you cast a fly too long over a rising trout and then draw your fly line back clumsily over its head you run the risk of 'lining' the fish. Trout which have been lined become spooked and may well disappear from view reluctant to rise again until you have moved on. If you think you may have lined a trout often the best recourse is to rest the area for half an hour or so and then return with a more cautious approach.

Lines
Rod and line fishing has been around since Roman times and the materials used to make a fishing line ranged through braided thread, *horsehair* and silk to modern slick coated polymers with a braided nylon core. See also *floating, intermediate* and *sinking lines*. In the old days lines were continuous length sometimes braided or tapered to a point and notably this was so of the horsehair line which got down to a single strand of hair on to which was tied the fly. Today lines are manufactured with weighted *tapers*. These will take the form of either a WF (weight forward) taper which adds extra weight at the front end of the line or a DT (double tapered) line which has the bulk of the weight of the line in the mid section. The former is designed more for distance and the latter for more delicate presentation at shorter range.

Lochs

In Scotland, inland freshwaters are called lochs rather than the English term lakes or the Irish term loughs. A number of seawater lochs also exist though the fishing is very different in these when compared to inland waters. Freshwater lochs can be classified as eutrophic (mineral rich), mesotrophic (less rich but still with reasonable plant growth) and oligotrophic (mineral poor, often deep and acidic in nature). See also *brackish* and *machair*. When visiting Scotland note the correct pronunciation of loch is with a throat clearing 'huch' at the end its not 'lock' which is something into which you insert a key. A particular style of fishing has evolved to cope with fishing on large stretches of freshwater, see *Loch Style*.

Loch Ordie

The bushy Loch Ordie is one of the old order of UK *dapping* flies. It's a versatile wingless fly which can be fished semi-static as a dry fly, employed as a wake fly on floating line with fast retrieve or fished sunk. While it is meant as a general insect representation it can be exceptionally useful on windy days as a sedge or mayfly on the surface or fished sunk as a darting shrimp. Size 10 to 14 are the norm for the Loch Ordie and its dressing is fairly simple with the body comprising almost totally of hackles palmered over a bed of tying silk. Hen hackles should be tied in to slope away from the head of the hook. Though there are variations the tying in sequence is usually black hen first followed by dark ginger followed by white. This is one of those vague patterns which tends either to illicit a head over heels response from trout or be studiously ignored, there is not much in the way of half measures here.

Loch Style

Loch style is an old tactic of fishing teams of flies from boats on stillwaters notably Scottish and Irish lochs/loughs but its use is widespread throughout the UK. Effective loch style (sometimes termed *traditional* fishing) usually needs a good breeze and a wave on the water. A team of flies on *droppers* (usually two or three but as many as a dozen have been used in the past) is cast out on a long rod (10 to 11ft is ideal) and then retrieved back with the rod tip parallel to the water. Just before lifting off the rod tip is raised up causing the top dropper to come up to the surface and skip across the wave. This creates a wake fly and the trout can be excited by this scurry and make a grab either at the top fly itself or turn down on one of its followers. Loch style can also be executed from the bank with good results, it is not the sole preserve of boat fishing.

Loop

As the line travels back and fore in the air during a casting sequence a

Loch style fishing. Geoffrey Bucknall gets to work.

U-shaped loop is formed above and parallel to the angler's head. A tight loop is desirable as a fat, floppy circular one is liable to result in a poor, uneven execution of the cast. To make a tight loop a reasonable amount of line speed must be generated by using the rod as a lever to *aerialise* the line crisply. If the timing goes wrong the end result will be a stuttered, splashy cast.

Lure

In the UK lure fishing normally involves using a longshank wet fly (size 6 to 10) fished on an intermediate or sinking line with a medium to fast retrieve to stimulate an aggressive response in stocked stillwater rainbow trout. The lure often looks like a fleeing fish, those *Streamers* of the US are roughly designed to do the same thing. Normally this will be done in deeper water where fish are lying low without visible rises. Older versions of lures are the longshank designs of the *Dunkeld* and the *Butcher* which were known in the 1800s as 'fancy flies'. Popular modern lures include the Dog Nobbler, the Viva, *Ace of Spades* and many others.

Machair

On islands off the west coast of Scotland (Inner and Outer Hebrides) the fertile semi-flat strip of land between freshwater lochs and the sea is called machair. Machair land is largely sand-based but is still very rich as it has a calcium base of ground-up shell deposits. It will harbour a rich variety of plants and wildlife. Machair lochs are almost exclusively found on the Hebrides and the shallow water in these will have a higher than average salt content. Their alkaline nature means an excellent growth rate for resident browns and migratory sea trout. Usually the water is very clear with a pale sandy bottom which means a dull overcast day is the best time to catch fish.

Management of Trout

The management of wild trout differs from the management of a commercial stocked fishery which is using hatchery-reared fish. Providing a wild trout population has a reasonable balance of fertile female and male fish, a reasonable food supply, cool, clean well oxygenated water and adequate access to spawning redds which contain non silted *gravel*, then generally the trout will get on with it. Management in this case needs to be a monitoring situation with perhaps the occasional helping hand in habitat management for example clearing out clogged up redds. *Catch returns* for wild fish populations are notorious for lack of precise

A machair loch of the Scottish Hebrides.

information however they can provide a bit of guidance as to how the water is faring generally. Management of stocked fisheries is a more precise art with clearer statistics of what is put in and what is taken out. In both cases however the weather can play a crucial role. Very hot weather for example will be indiscriminate in deoxygenating wild or stocked waters and causing fish kill.

Marabou
Marabou plumes are the instantly recognisable soft, long, almost mushy feather used principally in many rainbow trout *lures* in the UK. Wet marabou acts as a soft pulsing material sub surface which trout can find attractive. Popular flies employing a marabou feather include the Damsel Fly Nymph, Black Cat and the Viva.

Marbled Sedge
This is a beefy caddis fly with a flecked brown and grey roof-shaped wing. In the UK it is mainly a river insect but there are hatches on stillwaters provided that the base of the lake is gravel rather than mud. For a caddis fly its quite a pretty insect and standard imitations for the hatched version would be an Adams or a Silver Sedge.

Marbled Trout
The marbled trout (Marmorata) is a very distinctively marked trout at one time found only in the remoter rivers of Slovenia (Yugoslavia). Because of pollution and hybridisation with introduced trout it is now almost totally confined to the Soca River where sterling work has been done to preserve an almost extinct strain of trout. The greenish flanks marbled with black lines are the give away feature of this trout, and it is somewhat similar to the *lake trout* but with jagged stripe markings rather than spots. Small marbled trout have a predominantly insectivorous diet but upon growing they soon take up a *ferox* type fish eating role and consume the local *grayling*. This abundant source of protein makes their weight shoot up and Marmorata are sometimes caught on big *lures* in the teens of pounds. Strong leaders and a steely nerve are required for this type of fishing as these bigger trout only appear at dusk to chase the grayling.

March Brown
The March Brown is a well known fly fairly common in fast flowing rivers in the UK. Its main hatches are early in the season and with its prominent upright wings, the March Brown almost always acts as a trigger in getting overwintering trout to feed on the surface. Imitations of the March Brown can be used universally to represent a variety of upright winged insects. Dry, wet and nymph versions of the March Brown are popular multi-purpose

Marabou flies.

flies. The dry March Brown is especially versatile and a favourite dressing is one by W H Lawrie with a mixed yellow seal's fur and hare's ear body, fine gold wire rib, tail of honey dun cock hackle fibres, upright wing hen pheasant and head hackle of henny brown. This is a reasonably buoyant fly but a smear of floatant might be required in fast water.

Marl

Marl is a pale clay-like lime-bearing mud commonly found in various waters (predominantly lochs) in the counties of Caithness and Sutherland in the far north of Scotland. Lochs containing marl will have a higher degree of alkalinity and in general terms the feeding for trout will be much richer than in stony or peat-based acidic lochs. Waters containing marl can be said to be *limestone* lochs and they frequently have a profuse hatch of Green Drake *mayfly* as the large nymphs of these insects make their burrows in the firm but penetrable marl.

Match the Hatch

Matching the hatch is a peculiarly European term. North American anglers tend do it semi-automatically without thinking about other fly types and tactics, whereas the British draw distinctions between imitating locally profuse insects and using a vague general representation. There is no doubt that it is an ancient tactic found throughout Europe as the earliest fly fisher of the Roman Empire records matching his fly to a locally hatching fly on a stream near his home.

Mayflies (North America)

In the US most upright winged flies small, medium and large are classed as 'Mayflies' with no distinction between them. This means everything from a Blue Winged Olive to a Green Drake falls into this category though thankfully there is some distinction made in named dressings. This differs from the UK's classification of mayfly and can be a source of some confusion.

Mayfly (UK)

In Great Britain the mayfly hatch is the real thing i.e. big Green Drakes galore. They are one of the largest insects trout can consume with prominent upright lacy wings and three tails. Density of the mayfly hatch depends on location. Not all freshwater systems contain these luscious insects but mayfly can be found from the Hampshire chalkstreams to the lochs of Caithness and Sutherland. Survival of mayfly depends on adequate clay-like soil being present in the watercourse as this is where the mayfly nymph makes its burrow. It is important that this does not dry out with fluctuating water levels as the nymph may live for up to two

Mayfly (UK).

years within this burrow. For this reason mayfly are not normally present on stony rivers and lakes where there is no appropriate nymph habitat. The length of the hatch ranges from a 'duffers' fortnight' in southern England to a two month long hatch in the northern highlands. UK mayfly will usually begin to appear from late May onward floating up to the surface in droves. Once near the water surface the nymph wing case splits and the beautiful mayfly open their wings like little sailboats and float down on the breeze. They will then flutter off to dry their wings on the nearby undergrowth for perhaps two days before mating and ultimately dying falling as spent spinners. This dramatic life cycle means the trout have a field day taking the mayfly with gusto in the ascending nymph stage, or as winged insects struggling on the surface or as dead or dying spent flies. Mayfly imitations can be either purist in nature or very vague representations of a big struggling insect. F M Halford's Detached Body Mayfly has never been bettered but flies like the *Adams*, *Grey Wulff*, *Hoppers* and *Golden Olive Bumbles* all work well in a breeze.

Memory
When you first draw the fly line off the reel to begin casting the line may retain some memory. Older, poor quality lines virtually corkscrew like wire when stored for any length of time on the reel and take an age to

straighten out if at all. This makes your attempts to cast extremely clumsy. Thankfully modern fly lines are now manufactured with materials with low memory retention though you will still need to go for the best line you can afford. Regular cleaning and treating as well as changing your line every year to two years should ensure you avoid memory or at least make any memories in your trout fishing happy ones.

Mend Line
When you 'mend' line you effectively straighten it and/or put the fly line behind the path of the fly. In river fishing when a cast across the flow is made the current may push a belly in the line forward at such a pace the fly does not have time to swim properly. To avoid the trout looking at the line first rather than the more important fly, mend the line back upstream by drawing a semi-circle with the rod tip in a direction contrary to the flow. In stillwater fishing you may still need to mend line if the wind is pushing a big bend into your line as you try to retrieve it. Hooking a fast-taking fish is often more difficult if you have to pick up a great bulge in the fly line before making a firm contact.

Micro Patterns
While a considerable number of fishing terms do not mean exactly what you first think, micro patterns are indeed very small versions of flies often made to imitate specific food a trout might eat. These tiny flies are tied in nymph, wet or dry style but be warned, you need nimble fingers and a lot of patience to achieve a subtle result.

Midges
Midges belong to the *chironomid* family and they form a critical part of the UK's trout diet. These are flat winged flies and they range from the very small biting variety (Scottish midges hatching in profusion are liable to send sane men mad) to the bigger versions like the Large Green Midge. Because they are not the most notably glamorous of insects, by comparison mayfly and olive have stately upright wings, they have in the past been ignored especially by fly tyers determined to create the ultimate dry fly. In Scotland *traditional* flies have for centuries been used to imitate the huge range of midge however since the growth in popularity in stillwater fishing across the UK more attention has been paid to some exact representations. *Bloodworm* now have several semi-exact imitations as do midge pupa in the form of Suspender *Buzzers*. The winged hatched midge can be imitated with anything from a *Black Gnat* or a small *Kate McLaren*.

Migration
It is often assumed there is a distinct difference between a *migratory*

trout and one which lives its entire life in freshwater. In actual fact there is a considerable blurring at the edges around this assumption. Most trout in waters not linked to the sea will still try and migrate to inflowing small streams in order to spawn. Wild brown trout will actively migrate round lakes toward their natal stream usually in late September. Trout in either flowing or stillwater will also migrate toward an abundant food source which might only appear for a set period of time. This phenomenon occurs at *mayfly* (Green Drake) hatch time when trout will travel toward the most prolific hatch areas and almost queue up to enjoy the carnival.

Migratory Trout

In the US migratory brown trout are known as sea trout while migratory rainbows are known as steelheads. The same is true for the former in the UK however there are very few rainbows migrating to the seas surrounding the British Isles. This is mainly due to the non-native stocked rainbows of the UK being largely grown in hatchery ponds without any genetic memory imprint of their natal spawning streams. Migratory (sea) trout are the same species as brown trout only they have chosen to go to sea. Research in the UK has indicated that a higher proportion of female to male trout run to the ocean seemingly more aware of the urge to feed up in time for spawning. Male trout on the other hand appear more territorial, lingering in the natal river as big brown trout fighting off invaders. As the young trout travel to the sea they become smolts and their full silvery coat appears once they have spent time in the salt water. Immature sea trout may spend up to five years at sea in shoals swimming around the coastal waters feeding and growing fast until it is time to make the journey back to their natal stream. Once they have spawned they may drop back to sea as mature trout in order to recover (see also *Kelts*). Mature fish may spawn several times during their lifetime.

Minnows

Minnows are a species of small fish which can form a staple part of the diet of trout. They may be an indigenous fish as in some North American or English waters but they can also be an invasive non-native species introduced by bait fishers as is the case in numerous Scottish lochs. Typical minnow imitations include *streamer* patterns in the US and shiny *lures* in the UK. See also *Sticklebacks*.

Molluscs

Freshwater dwelling trout are avid consumers of molluscs notably snails and pea mussels. Sea trout may also consume limpets if they can access them. Molluscs are easy prey as they are slow moving semi-static creatures needing little or no chasing and consequent expenditure of energy. Molluscs are also present in the aquatic environment all year

127

round and provide much needed nourishment when surface hatches are scant. Though snails and pea mussels are encased in shells this offers little protection from hungry trout who simply consume them shell and all. The trout's digestive tract is sufficiently robust for the shells to pass through and there are also strong digestive juices present which slowly break the shells down. Trout like the *Gillaroo* have a serious snail consumption and have specially thick stomach walls. It is easy to detect snail-feeding fish as their bellies often feel full of little stones which are actually snail shells.

Monofilament

Monofilament is just another name for nylon made from a single continuous rather than braided strand. See also *leader*. Mono comes in different breaking strains which differ between North American ratings and British ones. In the UK BS 3 to 5lb is standard to fish for trout unless they are particularly fierce heavyweights in which case a BS of 6 to 8lb is used.

Movement of Prey

All trout detect their prey by the way it moves in the water. Trout use a combination of senses to find their lunch. Ears and eyes are employed and they also use the additional power of their *lateral line* which detects vibration in their immediate area. As long as the movement of your fly does not look abnormal, suspicious and/or scare the trout you are in with a shout. You can improve your fish catching considerably by fishing the fly on an appropriate speed of retrieve: slow for nymphs fast for lures and so on. Interestingly if a trout is described as 'moving' it means it's a *taking* fish busy feeding on something.

Mucous

Trout have an important film of slippery mucous over their scaly skin. This acts as a protection in extreme conditions notably very hot or very cold weather when it acts as an extra layer. Trout also develop thicker mucous prior to spawning though this is also associated with the onset of a cold winter. When handling fish with the object of returning them it is best to wet your hands as this stops friction damaging the mucous film. Also when using a landing net it is important to use fine knotless mesh which does not pull off too much of this essential natural protection.

Muddlers

Muddlers are virtually unsinkable wake flies which are designed to imitate struggling caddis flies or similar large insects on the water surface. They are fished on a medium to fast retrieve and if the trout are lying just sub surface the Muddler will almost certainly attract their attention. *Deer hair* is the main constituent in making Muddlers. It is used at the head of the fly where it is trimmed into a cone shape. Often there will be a few strands of deerhair also used in the wing all of which makes for an extremely buoyant fly. Common Muddler flies are the Muddler Minnow, Black and Silver Muddler and the Mini Muddler range.

Native Trout

There are basically three types of trout throughout the world. These are native, wild and stocked. Native trout are fish which have seen no intervention from Man in any way. A typical example of 'intervention' is stocking native trout waters with genetically different trout. Native fish have for generations been spawning and dwelling in the same habitat and they will carry all the appropriate *genes* necessary to survive there. In the UK true native populations of trout are in short supply as hybridisation with

A native trout of Loch Watten, Caithness about to be released.

introduced trout has corrupted the gene pool. However there are still a few native trout living above impassable waterfalls in Scottish highland streams and similar untouched water systems. *Wild trout* may still carry some of the ancient genes but the majority are hybridised fish, the offspring of native trout spawning with introduced stock. Note that since wild trout spawn in natural conditions they are not the same as *stocked trout* which are born and reared in tanks and ponds before being introduced into a new aquatic habitat.

Natural(s)
If an angler tells you 'they are taking the natural' then it simply means that trout are preoccupied with feeding on the indigenous insect appearing locally. This means you have two options either *match the hatch* fairly exactly with your carefully chosen fly or hope you can intercept the trout with a general representation and stimulate an aggressive response. Patterns like the Blue Winged Olive or the Green Drake are used when exact imitation of a local hatch is required whereas British flies like the *Dunkeld* or the *Zulu* cannot really be classed as copies of the real thing.

Needle Fly
The needle fly is at first glance a small rather insignificant insect of the Stonefly family. However in stony, less rich rivers and lakes around the British Isles they can provide a fair bit of nourishment for trout especially early and late in the season. The Connemara Black or a *Black Gnat* imitation also doubles as a needle fly in stillwater fishing while anything sparse and black does the trick on rivers when these are hatching.

No-See-Ums
This is a rather good term from North America used to describe tiny hatching flies which are for the most part impossible to tie as an exact representation. Typical No-see-ums are not much bigger than a caenis or reed smut but despite being minuscule, trout can at times become fixated upon them gobbling them up as a sort of soup rather than picking them off as individuals. Size 22 imitations might just begin to get there but a dense hatch of these tiny flies is often a wet blanket on otherwise productive fishing.

Nose
Trout do have a vague sense of smell, not in the human league but nostrils are present nonetheless. In murky water trout will often pick up on a *trotted* worm far quicker than a carefully cast fly. This appears to be because they 'smell' the chemical liquids (blood and mucus) exuding from

the worm as it squirms on the hook. Fish will also 'nose' incoming freshwater streams in order to try and recognise the distinct odour characteristics of their natal streams. It is rather like the wine merchant looking for the perfect 'nose', they instinctively know when it's the right one to run up and spawn.

Nylon
Leaders, tippets, monofilament call it what you will but nylon makes the connection between fly and fly line. Most modern nylon is very good quality and as long as it is stored out of bright sun which weakens its strength, you should have no particular problems with it. When adding droppers it is important that the joining knots do not weaken the holding capacity of the nylon, wind knots have the same effect. Anglers sometimes talk of 'smash' *takes* breaking the nylon. In actual fact this is unlikely and it is normally the knot in the nylon will slip and the fish depart with a fly in its jaw. Clean breaks only occur when the fish rubs the nylon hard on a sharp rock and effectively snaps himself free. Its important that the BS matches the type of fish you are seeking. Larger sea trout might need 8 to 10lb while small wild browns are normally OK with 4lb BS.

Nymph Fishing (Rivers)
Techniques of fishing the nymph upstream in rivers were around for some time before the Skues period of 1880 to 1940 however it is his name that is most associated with this tactic. It's a simple style of casting the nymph upstream ahead of the prospective trout and then letting it drift back with a raised rod tip keeping as much of the fly line off the water as possible. Skues was modest enough to admit he discovered upstream nymph almost by accident as he had purchased some pretty useless dry flies which refused to float well. He observed trout taking this inefficient fly beneath the surface and a 'new' technique was born. You need good *hands* in order to feel for any trout taking the nymph as it trundles along in the current, essentially it is wet fly fishing executed upstream rather than *across and down*. By raising and lowering the rod tip slightly you can sometimes *induce* a trout to take the nymph by giving the fly a more natural looking movement in the water.

Nymph Fishing (Stillwaters)
Sparse wet flies fished slowly in stillwaters can be said to imitate nymphs and this type of fishing has been going on since time immemorial. Modern techniques with *Buzzers* fished on slow retrieve just below the surface are broadly used to imitate midge pupa and natural nymphs. Fishing nymphs in teams of two or three in stillwaters is particularly effective on hard, bright days and also in semi-calm conditions when standard wet fly is not

producing the goods. An intermediate line can be used for extra depth. With no current to move the nymphs a slight rise and fall of the rod tip creates the impression of a natural nymph as it slowly stutters to the surface.

Nymphs (Artificial)

The earliest artificial nymphs belong to the sparse *Spider* variety popularised in the UK in northern England and the Scottish Borders from the early 1800s on. Flies like the Snipe and Purple or Partridge and Orange are excellent nymph representations. Traditional nymphs are always made without a wing either as a shaped body or shaped body with very sparse hackle at the head of the fly. Nymph representations can be made in different weights with correspondingly different sink speeds. They range from heavyweight *Czech Nymphs* to lighter versions like the Gold Ribbed Hare's Ear. Popular nymphs today include the Pheasant Tail Nymph, Mayfly Nymph, Olive Nymph and others.

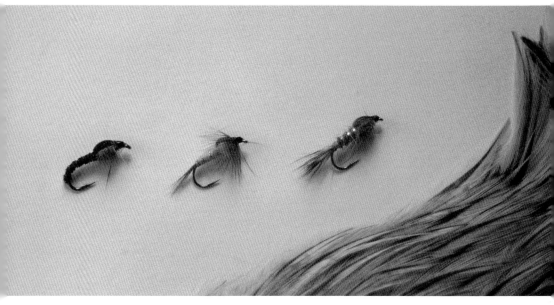

Nymph (Artificial).

Nymphs (Natural)

Nymphs are the aquatic stage of an upwinged fly, the bit between larva and hatched dun. Midge pupa are sometimes classified as nymphs especially by stillwater fishermen however strictly speaking nymphs are a separate stage in a fly's development. They come in four differing forms: burrowing, crawling, swimming and flat nymphs. Of these the burrowing nymph is probably the most important as it encompasses *Mayfly* (Green Drakes). Swimming nymphs include the Pond and Lake Olive as well as the Blue Winged Olive. Nymphs provide excellent cannon fodder for hungry trout as their movements are ponderous and they are vulnerable to attack either on the river/lake base and/or as they make their way to the surface.

Oak Fly
In the UK this is an ancient species of terrestrial born fly rather ignored by anglers despite the fact that the colours used in its dressing are common to many modern patterns. The natural insect is reasonably big with an orange and brown striped body and it provides a meaty mouthful for trout early and late in the season. The traditional dressing given in Courtney Williams' *Dictionary of Trout Flies* has a body of orange floss, tail of red hackle strands, *Coch Y Bondhu* hackle and woodcock wing. This is a really nifty fly for stillwaters where there is plenty of fish activity either on or just below the surface. The Orange Invicta could loosely represent an Oak Fly as could the *Zulu* with an orange tag rather than a red one. It is an excellent if underrated pattern.

Olives
Olives are profuse hatching insects with prominent upright wings and two tails. They are also known as mayflies in the US however in the UK we give true *mayfly* (Green Drakes with three tails) a separate billing. Olives are common throughout the UK and the US and form a staple part of the trout's diet. Some of the most familiar to river anglers are the Large Dark Olive, Medium Olive, Pale Watery and Iron Blue and these play a vital role in getting trout to rise. On lakes and lochs the Pond and Lake Olive are equally important trout attractors. Trout take olive nymphs, hatched olives on the wing and spent flies with gusto. Imitations of olives are legion with amongst many others the Greenwell's Glory, Rough Olive, Olive Quill and Wickham's Fancy strong contenders in the UK. The GRHE is an excellent imitation of the olive nymph.

Orange
When UK fly patterns were first constructed with orange in them (probably early 1800s) a number of leading lights in fishing scoffed at them calling them *fancy flies* not worthy of *educated* trout. The argument was that bright orange patterns did not imitate anything standard and were therefore not a patch on natural looking dry fly and/or nymph. This assumption was ill founded however for nature is far more colourful than

first supposed. Freshwater shrimps which trout consume in abundance can have organic orange material clearly present in their bodies and sticklebacks (small UK fish) have an orange flash on their flank when ready for mating. Bearing this in mind it is not surprising some of the most successful loch patterns include orange in their make-up to help stimulate a feeding as much as an aggressive response. These include amongst others the Kingfisher Butcher, Dunkeld, Oak Fly, Orange Invicta, Doobry and Grenadier.

Overhead Cast

The overhead is the standard cast used by the majority of fly fishers. Technical descriptions of its execution only began to appear with the advent of more modern materials like silk then nylon-coated fly lines which allowed the line to flow easily through its guide rings. Prior to that casting was almost certainly a wind assisted affair with the fly or flies on tapered horsehair lines simply pushed out by the wind behind and *dapped* on to the water with the aid of a long rod. *Reels* to store line seem to first come on the scene in the mid 1600s but it seems the basic

Overhead cast.

overhead cast did not really amount to much other than hoisting the whole caboodle aloft and then letting the wind do the rest. By the mid 1800s the overhead was being described as throwing the fly by means of 'a sweep or curve round his head'. Today there is a myriad of technical books on how to execute the perfect overhead however the basic principle of starting low, smoothly lifting the rod to the vertical line to accelerate the line aloft then allowing it to stretch out behind before a high forward tap propels the line out, is the norm.

Oxygen

Trout need oxygen to survive and they absorb it from the water through the gills situated at each side just below the head. As the water flows over the gill filaments oxygen is taken in and carbon dioxide expelled. Trout need a reasonably high oxygen content (saturation) in the water in order to thrive, rainbows cope a little better with deoxygenation than browns but this is generally an oxygen rich species. In prolonged periods of hot weather, waters will lose some of their oxygen content while their CO_2 content increases. In these adverse circumstances trout become torpid and if oxygen is not replaced they may die. This is particularly the case in overheated sheltered stillwaters or slow moving streams which stagnate without wave action or sufficient flow respectively.

Palmer

The history of how this term first came into use is a fascinating one. Palmered originally meant wrapped or wound around and is thought to date to the Holy Wars when soldiers returned bearing or possibly wearing palms and also from Medieval plays when Mummers (actors) wrapped themselves around in twigs and brush. The famous *Soldier Palmer* still in frequent use today appears to stem from these very ancient times. Then during the 1600s various fishing luminaries including Venables and Walton make frequent reference to trout consuming 'palmer' worms. While this was often assumed to be hairy caterpillars it could also be an old term for caddis larvae crawling along wrapped inside their case. Certainly the 'palmer worm' was also known as the 'pilgrim' with a nomadic lifestyle. It is good to think this antiquated term is still fresh with palmered flies as popular as ever. In fly dressing terms a palmered fly is one overwound with hackle along the length of the hook and not just at the head. Important flies featuring this technique today apart from the Black and Soldier Palmer include the Zulu and Bumble series along with a host of other *wingless wonders*.

Parachute

Parachute hackles are tied on to the top of the hook shank in a neat circle in order to make the fly float better. They have been around for a comparatively short time in fishing terms only appearing in both American and British fishing literature in the early to mid 1900s. The idea behind this type of fly dressing is to make the presentation of the fly to the waiting trout as soft and as natural looking as possible. The parachute effectively slows the descent of fly on to water as well as making it sit up and beg a bit more. Parachute tyings seem considerably more popular in the US than Britain where numerous already successful dry flies also come in parachute versions for example the Parachute Adams, Parachute Black Gnat and Parachute Blue Dun.

Parr

Small young trout between the fry and adult stage are known as parr. Non-migratory trout pass through the parr stage directly into adulthood whereas migratory sea trout go through the smolt transition before maturity. Parr will have developed enough to fend for themselves away from the natal stream and the sheltered fry environment. They are often caught by anglers in May and June as they are still in the greedy growth stage and will aggressively compete for any food including artificial flies which come their way. Parr are perfectly formed little trout complete with a greyish thumb print marking along their flanks. These characteristics can sometimes be retained into adulthood, see also *Parr Marked Trout*. The actual term parr may stem from the old Scots word 'par' which seemed to mean a small trout but it could have been confused with char, see also *Arctic charr*. The extra 'r' on parr was a frequent English corruption of old Scots words.

Parr Marked Trout

Parr marked trout are the same species as brown trout. During the days of the British Empire the Victorians had a penchant for classing trout by many different names this being one which relates to the fishes' markings. The natural historians of that era were quite right to draw attention to these unusual markings however they got it completely wrong in declaring them a different species and caused endless confusion in the ranks. Today in the UK it is still possible to catch trout which have retained their parr markings right into adulthood. These are particularly beautiful fish with grey fingerprints along their flanks amidst black and red spots. It is now thought that these trout are more aggressive than their brethren and use the markings both as a 'come hither' signal to potential females at spawning time and as a 'keep off' sign to marauding males in their vicinity.

Parr marked trout.

Peacock Herl

Peacock herl comes from the black/green strands of the ornate tail feather of a peacock. It has a fine fuzzy green quality and makes excellent bodies for trout flies. Rather than being a solid black or a solid green colour peacock herl has a soft almost sparkly glint to it and this gives the fly a much more natural appearance. Typical UK flies employing this material include the Black and Peacock Spider which is a vastly underrated fly good on any stillwater and useful in smaller sizes on faster flowing rivers.

Pecking Order

All non-migratory trout have some form of pecking order present which means the most aggressive bigger trout hold the best territories in terms of food productivity and degree of shelter from predators. Smaller trout will come further down the pecking order and make do with lesser territories until such times as they can compete and edge out the big guys. When the larger fish are removed from the system altogether by anglers, predators or ill health the next in line simply move up and take their place. This

137

behaviour is seen in both still and moving water. Migratory trout tend to hold more shoaling patterns however that does not stop the most aggressive fish trying to be first in line for any morsels of food coming their way.

Pheasant Tail Nymph

The most famous version of the Pheasant Tail Nymph is probably the one tied by Englishman Frank Sawyer. It's a beautifully simple pattern yet it serves a multitude of purposes in imitating a wide range of olive nymphs

Pheasant Tail Nymph.

notably the large dark olive as well as nymphs of the claret and sepia dun and the iron blue. This fly can be used with equal success on both rivers and stillwaters. Its tying is easy with a tail of three cock pheasant fibres, underbody of copper wire shaped into a thorax hump at the head, overbody of pheasant tail wound on with copper wire tied fatter at the thorax, wing case pheasant tail fibres doubled over a few times at the head of the fly. The end result is a gently bulbous fly in classic nymph shape which sinks well in high water.

Plankton
In stillwaters planktonic crustaceans like *daphnia*, bosmina, cyclops and diaptomus can be regularly consumed by trout. These tiny creatures best viewed with a microscope are often known as zooplankton and/or water fleas. Some trout tend to fixate on these especially during peaks of abundance when the zooplankton is held within the water in dense clouds as during the first heavyweight daphnia blooms of May in the UK. Flies to imitate this type of plankton are impossible to devise however a bigger pattern cast in front of a daphnia feeding trout intercepts the feeding process and stands a good chance of hooking something.

Play
Once a trout is hooked it is necessary to play it in such a way that it stays on but with the minimum of stress before it is either dispatched for eating or released back into its habitat. To play a fish successfully you need to keep a firm tension on the line between you and the trout. This is usually done by keeping the rod tip vertical and retrieving and if necessary releasing line with your free hand until the fish is under control. Side strain may only be needed if the trout makes a sharp left or right turn straight for an obstruction on which to free itself. If a large trout jumps skyward it is advisable to dip the rod tip momentarily so as not to snap the leader and then quickly take up the slack again once the fish is back in the water. Heavier fish may also need to be played from the reel rather than trying to hand-line them in.

Pocket Water
Pocket water is an American term for those narrow, fast flowing, well oxygenated sections of river found in a canyon environment. These stretches will have deep runs cutting between the walls of the canyon and the water will have an almost white rapid appearance. The trout which dwell in these pockets are usually well protected from predators and can grow to a significant size. You will need a fair degree of physical fitness to tackle pocket water as it can only be reached by trekking over rough terrain, basically it is the place the less adventurous angler would usually avoid.

Playing a good trout in shallow water, Caithness, Scotland.

Pollution

The modern industrial age brings many unwanted damaging pollution incidents. Chemical spills into rivers, spawning streams and stillwaters can all have disastrous consequences on the resident fish population. In the UK, environmental agencies will issue fines according to the severity of the offence however these actions are often too little too late to save a fish population wiped out by careless and/or thoughtless practice. Legal cases involving industrial pollution incidents are frequently long drawn out affairs and by the time they are resolved the public eye is far less focussed on past environmental damage. As fish have no helping hand from the *cute factor* the eventual fine to the polluting business is often derisory, after all what are a few dead trout when the wheels of commerce need to be kept turning?

Predators

Trout have a wide range of predators. Fish-eating birds like divers (loons in the US), cormorants, goosander, osprey and heron chomp on a lot of trout as do mammals like the otter. Non-native feral mink are highly destructive of trout populations while water shrews and brown rats will plunder trout eggs if they get the chance. Bigger predatory fish like pike or even one of their own kind the *ferox* will also happily consume small trout. The most prolific if not the most skilled of trout predators remains man as an angler. Fishers predating with rod and line can do some damage to fish numbers especially if angling pressure is intense however methods like netting (illegal in freshwater in some countries) can wipe out a fragile population altogether.

Presentation

How you present a fly to a trout is going to have a direct influence on your ability to catch him. As long as your fly vaguely resembles a food item or looks like an invader to be aggressively chased and consumed, you are in with a shout. However it is that final throw when you actually get your fly near the trout which makes for a confident grab or a quick refusal. Good presentation is really all about not scaring the fish. Your fly and fly line must alight on the water reasonably gently, silence-shattering splashes and crashes are to be avoided. And it doesn't stop with getting the fly on the water, once there your pattern should be presented to the trout in such a way that it looks normal to him. This means fishing a nymph slowly at a natural pace and a lure fast as lures normally represent small fleeing fish. It is all about fooling rather than spooking the fish.

Priest

The priest is a small heavy implement used to dispatch trout quickly and humanely if the fish are meant for the table. Priests can be made of wood, metal or carved horn and will be of such a size as to slip neatly into an angler's pocket. Less familiar but no less useful is the fly named the Priest for example the Green Priest, Red Priest or Silver Priest. These are basic *spider* fly tyings with coloured shiny tinsel bodies and black hen hackle at the head. A few strands of red hen can be added as a tail but the fly seems to work well enough without this extra. The Green Priest is exceptionally useful on stillwaters as a midge or olive nymph representation while the Red or Silver versions are good general attractors on any water flowing or still.

Punkie

This is an obscure North American term for small midge-like flies. Certain types of *Chironomid* are given this name but as far as can be ascertained there is no exact imitation and *Black Gnats* should suffice.

Purist/Purism

Purism was born out of the dry fly cult of the late 1800s promoted by F M

Halford and many of his followers. If you were a purist it meant you would fish only upstream dry fly no matter the conditions, the venue and/or the time of year. To fish by any other method was seen almost as unethical. G M Skues was virtually blackballed from his local river for suggesting an upstream nymph might be more handy on certain days when no trout were rising. Scottish loch fishing with traditional wet fly was sneered at by the purists as an inferior technique with inferior flies. Today this may all seem rather silly and more to do with class snobbery than anything else which indeed it was, but at the time woe betide anyone who crossed the demarcation line and dared to try another method on the trout streams of Britain. Fortunately in the new millennium purism has almost died out but it has taken two hundred years or more for minds to broaden.

Put and Take

Heavily stocked fisheries were stock-reared trout are regularly added in and taken out, often on the same day, are known as 'put and takes'. This type of fishery is run on a tight commercially orientated budget with permit fees reflecting the amount of fish purchased for stocking. While put and takes cannot be classed as anything like wild fishing they do fulfil a need of sorts for those who want their fishing near at hand with relatively quick and easy fish to catch. They can also help ease the pressure on wild fisheries. In addition put and takes are also the ideal place to get an inner city child interested in fishing as the tyro will almost certainly catch something. The downside of this is the fact that they may then expect to catch something of similar proportion with the minimum of effort when they visit a (much more demanding) wild fishery. Disappointment will usually result from over inflated expectations built up from frequent visits to a put and take.

Quill

Quills are the longer tubular wing or tail feathers of a bird such as a pheasant, gull or hen. The feathered part of the quill i.e. the material stripped from along the hollow stem, can be used for a variety of purposes in fly tying. The feather fibres can be cut to size to make wings for wet or dry flies or in the case of something like peacock *herl* can be used for making an excellent fly body. Some artificial flies take their name from using the quill in their make up notably the Red Quill, Orange Quill or the Olive Quill.

Quotations

Fly fishing in general has produced some wonderful quotations over the years. The nature of our sport means that anglers are great at philosophising and history is littered with some wonderful bon mots. Right from the *Treatise* where Dame Juliana wrote 'It (the rod) will be light and full nimble to fish with' through to modern off the wall American writers of the twenty-first century like John Gierach – 'Mayflies in flight look like angels. Caddis flies look like moths on speed,' – there are some wonderful quotes. Others equally famed include Walton circa 1600s 'Angling may be said to be so like the mathematics, that it can never be fully learnt' or Cotton circa 1600 'To fish fine and far off is the first and principal rule for trout angling'. Skues circa 1920s came up with 'In nature nothing happens without a reason' which was an astute summary and a personal favourite. From the same era is John Buchan's eloquent summary of angling 'The charm of fishing is that it is the pursuit of what is elusive but obtainable, a perpetual series of occasions for hope'.

Rainbow Trout

The rainbow trout was originally exclusively from North America but after

Rainbow trout.

vigorous stocking movements it is now found worldwide. In the US rainbows can be classified under two separate descriptions, redbands and coastal rainbows. Redbands have the iridescent red/purple stripe along their flank while the coastals are a more dull grey colour. There can also be differences in characteristics between migratory rainbows also known as *steelheads* and the non-migratory lake dwelling rainbow. Some of the more colourful redbands can be likened to the spectacularly marked *Golden trout* and are quite stunning to look at. Coastal rainbows by comparison are a more dull grey, olive and silver shade with black spots. However considerable interbreeding between the two types has occurred often brought on by stocking policies and there are a considerable number of rainbow hybrids neither exactly coastal nor redband. Wild and well adapted rainbows allowed a roving lifestyle rather than those kept in pens are a wonderful sporting fish hard fighting and acrobatic. Sadly, in the UK some poorly thought out breeding programmes which go for quantity rather than quality, produce fish bred in such close captivity they have ragged fins and little stubs for tails. These grossly devalue the rainbow trout. There is simply no comparison between these apologies for fish and the wonderful wild rainbows of the US.

Rainfall

The amount of rainfall a river receives has a direct influence on the welfare of the fish contained therein. Too much rain especially if it falls in sudden monsoon-like bursts causes banks to collapse and damaging *spates* and/or floods are the result. Trout eggs and/or fry can be washed away and the habitat for mature fish gets turned into a brown soup for a while. Older trout seem to cope best with floods tucking themselves into any shelter they can find under banks or behind boulders so as to escape the worst of the excess flow. Too little rain is also not good as it will cause spawning areas and/or fry habitat to dry out resulting in many mortalities amongst young fish. Mature trout have to retreat to deeper areas of the river sometimes dropping right back to tidal water during severe droughts. A steady rainfall which allows the river to rise and fall at a natural rather than overly fast pace is best for trout as it allows them to adjust to any change of water quality. Unfortunately *climate change* in the twenty-first century is creating ever more unpredictable weather patterns with increasing numbers of feast and famine situations so that many rivers now experience unprecedented droughts and/or floods. Too much or not enough rainfall has similar effects on stillwaters however usually these are not quite so drastic especially if the lake is spring fed.

Reach Cast

The reach cast is common to the USA and is a style of upstream river cast which is said to cushion the fly against drag. An overhead cast is made in the usual way ahead of the prospective trout but just before the fly lands the line is pulled gently back towards the rod. This creates a little curl or loop in the line and allows the fly to travel back downstream without any unnatural movement. River anglers in the UK will also use this technique but not necessarily the term 'reach cast' when describing it. You need considerable sensitivity in detecting takes when using this looped line method and sometimes a *sight indicator* is used.

Red (in Trout Flies)

The inclusion of the colour red in a trout fly whether it's a red body, tail or hackle always seems to act as a stimulant to trout. Trout seem to take flies with a dash of red in them more out of aggression than they do a gentle feeding response. Red can send out an injured prey signal and trout tend to hit these imitations hard. Famous flies with that important dash of red in them include the *Zulu*, *Soldier Palmer*, *Bibio*, *Ke He* and Red Tag amongst many others.

Redds

Redds are the little gravel nests constructed by trout at spawning time. These redds once covered with gravel will harbour the deposited fertilised

Wild brown trout spawning on the redds.

eggs over the winter until they are ready to hatch out the following Spring. Redds are highly susceptible to *spate* conditions which can wash them away. Drought and/or hard frost conditions can also dry out redds and the offspring may die before incubation is complete.

Reel

The reel has a very long almost tortuous history in the UK. It first appeared in sporadic use during the 1600s however it seemed to tumble in and out of angling fashion until the mid nineteenth century when its every day use became fully established. Prior to employing reels, the line was simply tied on the end of the rod and the whole caboodle just dribbled over the water with or without wind assistance. Early reels were also known as 'winders' or 'winches' and these were little more than a crude wheel over which the line was wound. Thankfully advances in engineering meant that by the late 1800s fairly sophisticated reels made of brass or wood were to be found attached to most rods. Today we have endless trade name reels all claiming they are better than their competitors while in fact the basic engineering design for a fly reel has not changed that much.

Renegade

The Renegade is a top rainbow trout fly from the US which has now found its way into the fly boxes of many European anglers. Although principally designed for the rainbow trout it is an excellent general imitation for brown trout busy taking bigger midge. Its design is slightly incongruous with a beefy hackle at the head and again at the tail nevertheless the trout are usually eager to have a go at it. The dressing given by Jack Dennis in his book *Western Trout Fly Tying Manual* is gold tinsel tag, body of peacock herl, back hackle brown saddle and head hackle off white saddle.

Reservoirs

A reservoir is an artificial containment of fresh water used for local purposes be that drinking water or hydro electric power. Reservoir fishing has always been popular in the UK especially if the water is regularly stocked. *Rainbow trout* seem to do better in reservoirs than *browns*. The artificial raising and lowering of water height (see also *Dams*) often has a detrimental effect on the natural spawning facilities for brown trout. Rainbows are often stocked as sterile *triploids* and seem to adapt better. During the 1970s rainbow reservoir fishing took a giant leap in popularity in the UK and many new *lures* and *lines* were constructed to deal with this type of fishing.

Resting Trout

Trout do go through periods of inactivity when not engaged in feeding.

While this could not be classed as sleeping they definitely appear to be taking some form of rest. Early morning and late evening you will sometimes accidentally disturb a resting trout holed up in the shallows perhaps in only a foot or so of water. These fish will simply swim languidly away, they are not interested in feeding. It is interesting that a salmon resting up in a deep pool might sometimes be persuaded to take your fly while a resting trout will usually dismiss your efforts and turn away.

Retrieve
Novice anglers will sometimes assume that retrieving the fly is simply a way of bringing it back to you in order to cast out again. The retrieve is actually the part when you give your fly some life and it is therefore essential to impart an action which simulates the natural movement your imitation might make in the water. Thus the retrieve for a small nymph struggling to rise to the surface will be much slower than if you were stripping back a streamer which imitates a small fleeing fish fry. When fishing in flowing water it is necessary to retrieve enough to keep in good contact with the fly and to stop the line from bellying out in front of your imitation. In stillwater fishing there is no current and you must impart the appropriate movement to your fly. Varying the speed of retrieve is considered a useful stillwater tactic but its style has to be done according to what style of fishing you are using, e.g. dry or wet.

Rise
Trout rise up to the water surface to consume insects making anything from a resounding splash to the quietest of sips. When stalking trout as opposed to fishing randomly, the first thing an angler will normally look for is a rise. A rising trout is a taking fish, it is busy feeding on something and if you can get your fly quickly but gently in the vicinity you are in with a shout. Anglers will also talk of 'raising' a fish which means encouraging a trout to the surface to look at their fly. Though the fisherman may not actually hook the trout he has raised he has effectively brought on an artificial rise. When you hear the phrase 'fishing the evening rise' or less commonly the 'dawn rise' this is a collective angling term for a number of trout taking a semi-specific hatch.

Rise Forms
There are a number of classic rises to look for when fish are actively feeding. These include the head and tail rise, slash rise, gentle sip, the boil or simply a bulge in the water. All of these indicate feeding trout and you must get in the thick of it as soon as possible. Some anglers will go to great lengths to differentiate rises and what they might indicate in terms of

147

This trout has risen violently to the angler's fly and is dashing away sub-surface.

trout food. This is only really necessary when the trout are so pernickety as to keep rejecting your fly in favour of the natural.

River Trout

Trout populations which naturally regenerate in a particular river system will carry genes necessary to survive in that particular habitat. They may show behavioural characteristics unique to their river system. If their spawning areas are near to migratory fish redds the river trout may develop a salmon gene from accidental cross-fertilisation. This may give them a more migratory tendency and may increase growth rates in terms of overall size. Stock introductions over a lengthy period of time can dilute the original strain of trout and hybrids may result. River trout depend ultimately on an adequate flow of water for survival. Dams made by man or by beavers obstruct natural flow and climate change with their increasing number of droughts, place trout habitat under increasing threat.

Rods

The history of the fishing rod sometimes known as a pole, dates back to BC. Ancient Egyptians, Greeks and Romans all used fishing rods and certainly by the time the *Treatise* was written circa 1400s the use of a rod was extremely well established. Early rods were made in sections often using different types of wood spliced together. Hazel, juniper, fir, crab apple tree and greenheart were all used as rod sections, heavier wood at the *butt* and lighter on the top, and once everything was assembled a trout rod could be anything up to 18ft in length. Split (bamboo) cane rods only appeared on the fly fishing scene in the early 1800s and by this time the immense length of trout rod had been shortened to 10 to 12ft in length. Cane rods remained fashionable until the invention of lighter fibreglass materials in the late 1950s, fibreglass eventually being deposed with the manufacture of carbon fibre rods. Carbon rods are now the most universally favoured across the globe though a light wispy cane rod still has its aficionados.

Roll Cast

It seems likely the roll cast developed from an old cast known as the 'switch' which was a simple rolling over of the line without having to lift it overhead. Prior to overhead casting being developed anglers of old simply relied on the wind to blow out the line and probably occasionally used a form of roll cast. This simple style is particularly useful when there are obstructions like trees or high banks to the rear as the line does not travel behind the angler. To execute a roll cast the rod is simply turned to the side parallel to the water and then raised toward the head making a reverse D shape, before the line is rolled over in a circular motion back on to the water. Rather than the angler aerilising line the surface tension of the water is used to generate line speed.

Rollocks

In order to row a boat properly you need to slip the oars into holders called rollocks. These are shaped like upturned Us and stop the oar from sliding around as you row. An old gillies' trick if you do not wish a boat to be used without permission is to remove the rollocks and carry them with you rather than leaving them on the boat.

Run

In angling terminology there are two meanings to the word run. The first is when a big trout takes your fly and literally runs with it causing the reel to squawk as line is pulled out. The second is to do with river habitat. A run on the river is where the water (often at the tail of a pool) narrows into a fast rushing deep section. In warm weather trout will lie close to the run to gain maximum oxygen intake while in high water they may move to either side of it as the current may be too strong to maintain their *station* for any length of time.

Saltwater Trout Fishing

Fly fishing for trout in saltwater has been popular in the UK since the early 1900s. The principal quarry is the sea trout returning from its oceanic phase and about to enter its natal stream again. The Shetland Isles was particularly famous for its saltwater trout fishing until the 1960s when numbers of fish returning declined, see also *voes*. The art is still practised there and elsewhere around the UK coastline but the number of anglers participating in this branch of the sport has generally fallen perhaps coinciding with the rise in popularity of rainbow trout fishing. The technique involved is similar to stillwater trout angling with a selection of wet fly, lures and streamer patterns in size 8 to 12 employed on floating or intermediate lines with 6 to 8lb BS leader. You must pay attention to tide times as sea trout will tend to come in close to the shore to nose their rivers on the incoming tide. Some of the fish will run straight in on sufficient water while others will linger in shoals in the estuary. The principal diet of the sea trout is the *sandeel* though they will consume other small prey like crustaceans and small fish. Flies are therefore normally designed to loosely imitate this prey.

Sandeels

Sandeels form a major part of the diet of *sea trout* in its oceanic phase. They linger in shoals in the warmer saltwater of sandy estuaries and trout can sometimes be seen plunging madly amongst these creatures and giving them chase for all their worth. In recent years sandeel populations have declined in some parts of the UK mainly due to commercial over fishing however good numbers still exist along parts of the north coast of Scotland. Sandeel imitations are commonly fished in saltwater. Green, cream and white *Streamers* make excellent imitations of the sandeel which is about two to three inches in length with olive and silver cream tones.

Scissors

A commonly used phrase referring to how the trout was caught is to say he was 'Well hooked in the scissors'. The scissors are situated at either side of the trout's mouth and they do indeed look rather scissor-like being formed by the fishes' bony lip. To hook himself thus the trout must swim alongside the fly and then turn on it hard. The number of escapees you have from this kind of hook hold are usually less than a fragile hooking say on the lip or nose.

Scuds

Scud is a North American term for a nymph fly which resembles a freshwater shrimp. These are quite realistic in design and popular numbers include the Olive Brown Scud and the Flash Scud. Fished on a slow retrieve these patterns take trout when traditional wet fly is failing to come up with the goods.

Sea Trout

In the UK sea trout are simply *brown trout* which choose to go to sea. The inherited genes contained within each trout mean that some fish will be more determined than others to elope to the ocean if there is a suitable aquatic route. UK studies have shown it is often the females who have the strongest urge to run down river to go to sea. Their hormones are demanding that they feed up well in order to breed. The male trout on the other hand takes a more territorial stance and often has stronger inclinations to stay put and defend his patch in the river. As the brown trout descends its natal stream it will go through a *smolt* stage where its coat will become silvery and its body begins an adaptive process to enter saltwater. At sea the young fish (often known as *finnock*) enjoy much richer feeding, see also *sandeels*, and they will normally grow at a faster rate than when in freshwater. The sea trout may spend three to five years in the salt cruising along the coast in shoals usually following a defined route to different feeding grounds. Once mature it may weigh anything from 3lb to 10lb plus and the sea trout re-enters its natal stream to run up to spawn. Not all sea trout will run up to spawn every year, some will simply linger in the estuary in shoals and nose their natal streams but not enter them. These fish provide excellent *saltwater fishing*. Unlike salmon, sea trout may spawn several times during their lifecycle. In the US *rainbow trout* which take the migratory route spending up to half of their life in the ocean are known as *steelheads*.

Seals

Since the banning of the culling of seals without a licence in UK coastal waters, the seal populations have seen a huge growth in numbers. Seals predate on *sea trout* and Atlantic salmon in the fishes' migratory phase and can cause considerable damage to already depleted fish populations. It can be argued that seal predation is simply part of nature, seals have after all been there a lot longer than anglers fishing for sport. This

Fresh from the sea. These fish evaded seal predation but were caught by the angler's fly.

argument is fine if numbers of available fish keep in balance with the number of predators however the numbers of sea trout and salmon off the coastal waters of the UK has been steadily declining since the 1970s. Seals benefit immeasurably from the *cute factor* and ill informed animal rights activists can hamper any attempts to humanely cull seal numbers for the benefit of other species.

Season

In the UK the official *brown trout* season lasts from 15 March to 6 October however there are often local variations on opening and closing days. There is no close season for *rainbow trout* in Britain though some rainbow fisheries do close for a period during the winter months. In the US open and close seasons vary according to fish species present in the different states. Whether in Britain or North America it will usually be illegal to fish for and/or kill brown trout out of season. The close season was set up to allow wild trout to spawn and continue the species.

Sedge

In the UK the *caddis* fly is also known as a sedge. Trout feed on these throughout the insects' lifecycle. The grub within the cased caddis make a tasty mouthful of protein in winter, trout feed avidly on sedge pupae and will also take the hatched insect with considerable gusto. The mature sedge is easily recognised by its distinctive triangular roof-shaped wings and two long antennae at the head. When first hatched these insects have a habit of skittering across the water before taking flight and the trout taking a sedge will often make a distinctive slash *rise* usually designed to grab the sedge before it gets airborne. There are numerous different types

Sedge flies.

of sedge flies in the UK ranging from the quite large Great Red Sedge to the smaller Brown Silverhorn. Proven sedge imitations include the Silver Sedge, *Invicta*, Black Sedge, Shredge, *Wickham's Fancy* and Mini Muddlers amongst numerous others.

Shrimp (Artificial)

The design of artificial shrimp patterns ranges from very general versions like the *Soldier Palmer* right through to almost exact replicas made with translucent polythene backs, stubby legs and fuzzy bodies. Artificial shrimps are usually fished close to the bottom and will have some weight to them. Lead, tungsten or copper wire can be added to make the fly sink quicker. Normally imitations will have an olive, ginger, soft orange or reddish tinge to them. The Gold Ribbed Hare's Ear in size 10 to 14 makes a good shrimp imitation if you do not wish to go down the fiddly polythene coat route.

Shrimp (Natural)

Shrimps, also known as Gammarus, like a slightly alkaline environment, and do not thrive in acidic waters. They are found in both running and stillwater and spend their lives on or near the bottom usually close to weedy habitats where they feed on zooplankton. They can grow to just over a centimetre in length and tend to swim in a characteristic curling and uncurling sideways motion. Freshwater shrimps prefer a shaded environment and avoid bright light. They will be present all year in an appropriate water as opposed to having a particular season and trout will always feed avidly on these creatures if they get the chance. Where shrimps form a staple part of the diet the trout will develop a rich red/orange flesh. Shrimps are principally a translucent olive grey in colour, however depending on their diet they can also develop an orange or occasionally a blue spot in their middle section. These coloured spots will develop according to the diet of the shrimp for example shrimps feeding on a considerable amount of Diaptomus (a type of zooplankton) develop a prominent orange glow around their gut area.

Sight Indicator

A sight indicator is a small brightly coloured piece of wool or light plastic material usually coloured fluorescent pink or yellow, placed on the leader at a prescribed distance (about 2 or 3ft) above the tail fly. When you cast out the fly the indicator will float on or near the surface. If a fish takes the fly unseen beneath the water surface, the sight indicator will move and the angler should strike right away. This type of angling bears a close resemblance to coarse fishing with a float. In some quarters it is not

Shrimp (natural).

considered entirely sporting and may even be banned from the select few *purist* dry fly only venues in the UK.

Sink Tip
The sink tip is one of the oldest types of adapted *floating line*. The line will be weight forward or double taper with a length of heavier sinking line fused into the tip. The idea of this version is to let the fly fish deeper but still allow a swift pick up of line to recast. Full *sinking lines* plummet to the depths and need to be 'rolled' up on the surface before casting again. A sink tip does not go so far down so quickly and makes life that bit easier for the angler. See also *Ghost Tip*.

Sinking Line
When silk fly lines were overtaken by plastic-coated polymer versions it was found that by varying the type and density of the internal thread material, the line could be made to sink at different speeds. Sinking lines are sometimes required in deep, fast flowing rivers where the fly needs a

chance to swim nearer to the bottom and at reasonable speed. In fast currents a floating line gets whisked around at such speed the angler quickly develops arm fatigue and the trout barely have time to eyeball the fly before it is lifted off again. In stillwater fishing, sinking lines are predominantly used to tempt deeper-lying trout. In the UK rainbow trout fisheries are the main venue for using sinking lines, wild brown trout angling is normally though not exclusively floating line tactics.

Skunked

Skunked is a delightful Americanism for failing to catch any trout after a day's fishing. *Blank* means the same thing in the UK.

Slob Trout

This is now a largely out of date term for big *brown trout* which choose to linger in a brackish estuary environment. They are not sea going migratory fish but neither are they solely freshwater residents, rather they are trout which enjoy the best of both worlds. Slob trout can grow to 5lb or more depending on the quality and abundance of local feeding. They are fished for much in the way as you sea trout or brown trout and show a penchant for *streamer* type flies as well as traditional wet and dry fly.

Smolt

The young *sea trout* preparing to run to sea will go through a smolt stage. This is when the small trout begins to take on a silvered coat and goes from *parr* to growing adult. Smolts are the teenage years, not the baby and not the grown up but somewhere in between. Smolt size varies but usually they will be trout of about half a pound or so. Not only do the fishes' scales silver up, their gills also go through an adaptive process in order to cope with the change from fresh to salt water.

Smuts

Smuts or reed smuts are those tiny insects seen on the water surface. They are tiny dark flies resembling a minute version of a flat-winged house fly. Smuts are difficult to imitate because of their size and abundance. Your imitation would be just one amongst thousands. Some anglers try a *Black Gnat* when trout are 'smutting' but it can be a frustrating business as fish seem to fixate on these tiny insects and ignore artificial versions. Trout engaged on feeding on smuts make only a tiny *rise* little more than a sip.

Snails (Freshwater)

Some trout will tend to gorge themselves on snails if these molluscs are locally abundant either in still or flowing water. Snails are available all

Snails (freshwater) from the stomach of a trout.

year, which means they provide a valuable source of protein during the winter. It is interesting that some trout seem more prone to consume snails than others. The *Gillaroo* trout is a noted snail feeder with specially adapted stomach wall able to cope with the snail shells within. Snails go through periods of migration especially if the oxygen content of the water alters or it is mating time and during this time trout will actively feed on the molluscs. In the UK the most common types of aquatic dwelling snails include the Great Ramshorn, Small White Ramshorn, the Great Pond Snail and the aptly named Wandering Snail.

Snake Roll Cast

The snake roll is a modern variant of the *overhead cast* with an added twist of the wrist. It is an excellent way of quickly changing casting direction without having to do all that hauling in of loose line. The execution of it is relatively simple. The floating line is cast out in the normal way and then should a fish rise to the left or right, the line is whipped round in two circles by rotating the rod tip clockwise or anti clockwise in front of the body. As you see the fly line lift from the water and form into two circles you must lift the rod smartly vertical to the 12 o'clock position of a normal overhead cast position. This has the effect of rapidly aerilising the line and once the lot is airborne you can turn the body toward the new target and finish the forward cast in the normal way. Anglers using the snake roll cast gain a distinct advantage in being able to cover more rising fish with the minimum of water disturbance.

Snowfly

In the wild west of the USA notably the Rocky Mountain area you will often come across the oddly named Snowfly. It is actually a Black Midge pattern but gets its name from the winter hatches of midge seen on local waters. These *midges* often get stuck in some number in the snow at the edges of rivers and lakes hence the insect's confusing name. The pattern is simple but it must be tied in eye watering sizes 18 to 22 to be truly effective. Dressing is normally black ostrich herl for the body, black hen for the head hackle and a tail of a few fibres of dark moose hair.

Soldier Palmer

Along with the *Zulu* the Soldier Palmer (SP) remains one of the most successful trout patterns of all time. Principally used in stillwater fishing notably *loch style* the SP can be used to generally imitate anything from a *sedge* to a *shrimp* often being placed in the top *dropper* position. The history of this ancient fly dates back to the fourteenth century, possibly a good deal earlier. During the medieval Holy Wars soldiers returning to Britain would be wearing a uniform with a bright red cross on their chest. They would have ceremonial palms strewn at their feet to welcome them home, hence the flies name Soldier Palmer. The dressing is simple with a red wool body, gold wire rib and brown palmered hackle. The pattern should be made delicately enough to allow light and air to be trapped between the hackle fibres as this creates a slight shimmer sub surface which the trout find more attractive.

Sonaghen

The Sonaghen is a particular strain of trout found exclusively in Ireland. There is a noted population in Lough Melvin which spawns separately from the other trout notably *Gillaroo* and *Ferox* which also reside there. Sonaghen are generally a steely blue in colour speckled with black spots and very few red and they have black fins. They do not generally grow as large as Ferox or Gillaroo preferring to feed off smaller food items like midge larvae or zooplankton.

Spate

Rivers and streams which suddenly flood with high water after heavy rain are said to be in spate. Spates are normally associated with dirty water which will be carrying an extra loading of soil and vegetation washed off from the surrounding landscape. A spate which is fining down i.e. the water is clearing is said to be the best time for migratory trout and salmon fishing. The fish will have run up the river in the high water and should now be lingering in their favourite pools, that's the theory anyway. Spate rivers in the UK are not always as productive in terms of trout fishing as rivers fed from underground springs. Fluctuating water heights mean that trout habitat alternately dries out then floods and this can be destructive in terms of fish survival.

Spawning

In the UK wild *brown trout* will normally spawn anytime from late October through to early December. The urge to spawn is a powerful one. It compels brownies to migrate back to their natal stream and in large lakes/lochs, trout are known to travel over several miles to spawn where they were born. In rivers, trout will leave their normal mainstream haunts and run up small feeder burns or even ditches if the water height is sufficient. The main stimulant which pushes river and lake trout into the spawning streams is sustained heavy rain which produces a decent steady flow of water of sufficient depth. Changes in air and water temperature and even a full moon are also said to have an effect on the trout compelling them to try to run up to spawn. Successful spawning can only be achieved with clean *gravel* beds which provide reasonably stable *redds* for the fertilised eggs to be deposited in over winter. A common misassumption is that natural spawning is over in one go, far from it as brown trout will usually have several runs into their natal streams to pair off. This is to try and ensure the best survival rates of deposited eggs and the still-to-develop fry. If all offspring were laid down at exactly the same time and a severe *spate* or *frost* hit the stream then the next generation would be wiped out entirely.

Spey Cast

The Spey cast is normally associated with salmon angling but the first element of it is the very useful *roll cast* which is commonly used in trout fishing. This means the line does not travel behind and there is less risk of entanglements with high undergrowth behind.

Spiders

That famous Scottish border river trout angler W C Stewart circa 1850s is generally credited with inventing sparse wispy versions of wet flies

159

A delicate Spider pattern.

universally known as Spiders. Though these flies are themselves descended from earlier North country patterns it is Stewart who really brought them to the fore. Spiders were some of the first nymph style imitations in the UK, modern nymph fishing did not come on the scene until at least fifty years later. These sparse flies were originally meant exclusively for river trouting however they have a place in all types of fishing such is their versatility. They have very soft pliable hackles which fold up along the hook and then pulse in the current on retrieving. The flies have no wing and rely on a skinny body and sparse dressing to sink quickly in the stream. Stewart was a great advocate of delicate tyings and is forever remembered for tartly reminding his readers of 'the necessity of avoiding bulky flies'. Typical Stewart flies include the Black Spider, Red Spider and the Dun Spider. Of these Stewart declared the Black Spider 'the most killing imitation we know' though interestingly he credits James Baillie another local fisher of the period for introducing him to it. The dressing is body of brown tying silk and head hackle of cock starling usually tied in sizes 12 to 18.

Spinner

When a winged insect reaches full maturity and is able to reproduce it is known as a spinner. *Duns* are the immature adults while spinners are the insects with mating on their minds. Spinners mainly though not exclusively, will emerge in dancing clouds on calm summer evenings. *Olives* like the BWO or the Large Dark Olive produce immense spinner hatches. A spinner is not exclusively a fly fishing term however as metal 'spinners' can be used with appropriate rods when fishing for trout. Small waters do not generally benefit from spinning techniques as they have the effect of raking the water and spooking close together fish, however on large lakes with growing fish populations, spinning does not appear as detrimental.

Station

Trout in flowing water will use their fins to hold their position or 'station' in the current in order to access any food drifting down to them. Competition for the best stations will be fierce amongst trout of similar size especially *fry* and *parr*, however once the fish reach maturity, the big guys usually snap up the best stations and leave the rest in a loose *pecking order*.

Steelhead

The steelhead is a *rainbow trout* which has migrated to sea and then returned to its native freshwater river to spawn. It is common to various North American Pacific coastal waters particularly those of British Columbia, Alaska, Oregon, Washington and northern California. Steelhead are also found in the Great Lakes having been introduced into local rivers there during the 1800s. This trout has a steely blue-grey back and silver flanks while at sea but will lose its colour and revert to those characteristic rainbow crimson shades when in freshwater. They are a wonderfully energetic sporting fish much prized by anglers everywhere. Despite the propensity of rainbow trout in UK there are few if any surviving steelhead populations probably because the genetic make-up of tank reared rainbows does not encourage migratory tendencies.

Sticklebacks

Sticklebacks are found across the UK and grow to roughly the same size as *minnows* i.e. about one to two-and-a-half inches long, indeed the two species are sometimes confused. Some brown trout fixate on sticklebacks and can grow to considerable size when they consume this form of concentrated fish protein. The three-spined stickleback is the most common variety the other being the ten-spined stickleback and they normally have a silvery-olive colouration. The male stickleback develops reddish orange flanks when ready to mate and this acts both as a signal to potential mates and to help warn off rival males. Sticklebacks produce huge numbers of offspring and these are considered a pest when they take up feeding positions that young trout fry might otherwise enjoy.

Stillwater

Any inland freshwater lake, loch, lough, pond or reservoir can be considered a stillwater. Stillwater fishing for trout may involve different techniques from flowing water angling. In the UK there has been a dramatic growth in the popularity of stillwater fishing from the late 1970s onward principally for stocked rather than wild trout.

Stimulator

The Stimulator is a popular American fly designed to imitate larger insects like caddis/sedge fly stoneflies or mayfly. The dressing is bulky and buoyant and big rainbows and browns show no hesitation in crashing into it in the right conditions. Standard Stimulators are tied with olive or red bodies, an Adams-like hackle and elk hair wing normally in size 10 to 14.

Stocking

From the 1880s onward the introduction of hatchery-reared trout into freshwater systems became a principal fishery management tool right across the UK. Stocking was seen as a panacea for all ills, adding more trout into a water, whether it needed extra fish or not, was the accepted way to improve it. More trout equalled more sporting chances and it took until the 1960s or perhaps even later before angling clubs and fishery managers realised that heavy restocking could often do more harm than good. Important survival *genes* in *native* brown trout were forever corrupted by hatchery-reared browns during the rampant restocking ethos of the Victorian era. Adding rainbow stockies into a freshwater containing an established brown trout population can destabilise the resident browns who are not generally as competitive as the more greedy rainbow. Today a slightly more holistic approach is taken in wild fishery management with restocking not seen as an automatic first line of improvement. Restocking with locally reared brown trout bred from the same water is only encouraged if the natural spawning seems to be failing perhaps because of habitat degradation. Stocked rainbow trout fisheries in the UK can help take the angling pressure off wild fish and are to be commended in this respect.

Stocked Trout

Brown trout artificially reared in pens adopt different behaviour patterns to fish born and bred in the wild. Generally the longer the trout is kept in an artificial situation the more domesticated it becomes. Hatchery fish released into the wild when still in the fry stage can become naturalised over a much longer period of time and by the time they reach maturity some fish can appear not much different from the local brown trout. However trout kept for a long time in captivity say until two years old are less able to cope when released into the real aquatic world. Ronald Campbell, eminent fisheries biologist on the River Tweed in Scotland, described naturally spawning trout as 'wolves' while introduced tank-reared fish were 'poodles' and this description has rarely been bettered.

Stoneflies

Stonefly/Stoneflies are insects common to both sides of the big pond. They belong to the Plecoptera order with about thirty species to be found in the UK. They are hard-winged flies with four wings held folded flat above their bodies, stubby antennae and two equally short tails. They range in size from the Large Stonefly to the skinny little Needle Fly. Stoneflies thrive in well oxygenated stony habitats and are common to both rivers and lakes. They are consumed eagerly by trout especially if the olive or mayfly hatch is sparse. Stonefly nymphs provide a good gulp of protein especially in the early part of the season when natural feeding is otherwise scarce. The hatched variety of stonefly appears any time from late March reaching a peak in June. Most are a dull brown grey in colour but there is always an exception to every rule and the bright sprightly *Yellow Sally* is it in the stonefly family. Useful diverse imitations include the February Red, *Coch Y Bondhu* and the Large Stonefly. Snipe and Purple, Partridge and Orange or even the Gold Ribbed Hare's Ear take care of the nymphs.

Strap

A strap of flies is an old Scots term for a leader with several flies attached on it with *droppers*. The term is not much used now but is still occasionally heard on some of the more famous Border rivers like the Tweed or the Annan.

Streamers

In North America artificial flies dressed with long streamlined feathers akin to UK *lures* are known as streamers. These patterns are principally fish-like and are designed to be pulled fast through the water. Strikes will almost always be aggressive and you should use a reasonable strength of hook otherwise it can be straightened by a determined fish. *Rainbows*, *browns*, *steelhead* and *sea trout* will all have a go at these flies. In general the streamer wing should extend back over the hook up to a further hook length to effectively double the fly size. Wing materials vary from *marabou* to bucktail with a number made from badger or furnace hen.

163

Body materials will usually have an element of flash to them for example tinsel or mylar. The whole idea of a streamer pattern is that it looks like a small fleeing fish and easy prey for a marauding trout. *Purist* they ain't but still very effective in still and moving water.

Stress (in Trout)
Given that a trout's existence is very different from a human one where deep stress is commonplace, trout will still suffer from forms of nervous tension. Stress in fish can be caused from either social or environmental factors. Intense competition for food causes trauma and if it is an ongoing problem the trout may not thrive as well as it should. Equally the act of reproduction causes body stresses from which the trout may take a few months to recover. Stress can also arise from various environmental factors. For example sudden alterations in water temperature especially from cool to hot, *pollution* incidents and *spates* which alter water quality and speed of flow will all cause trout to suffer degrees of stress. In extreme situations especially those which cause deoxygenation of water trout mortalities can occur. Trout are undoubtedly a species which prefer the quiet life.

Strike
When a trout takes the fly the angler must lift rod and line to put tension between himself and the fish and effectively set the hook. This action is called striking the fish. Some anglers strike hard and fast for wild trout, so much so that sometimes they pull the fly away from the fishes' mouth. Strikes need to be timed according to how the fish takes a hold the fly. Aim to feel the fish and then lift into it. See also *Hooking a Trout*.

Strip
When you retrieve line back in with speed, the action is known as stripping line. Line can also be stripped off the reel to begin a lengthy cast but the term is more common for a fast retrieve. When you strip line the fly travels through the water with considerable pace and some trout notably rainbows, will give chase and thump into the fly. *Sea trout* and/or *steelheads* also like a stripped fly as it resembles a small fleeing fish which they are familiar with at sea.

Sulphur
In the US, certain types of yellow or olive mayflies (UK anglers might term them *Yellow Sally* or simply *Olives*) are sometimes called sulphurs. They are smallish insects reasonably common to both Eastern and Western streams. John Gierach recommends a neat imitation in the Sulphur Parachute tied in size 14 and 16. The dressing is fairly simple with a body of yellow dyed goose or turkey biot wrapped around the hook shank, wing

of a parachute post of light dun or white turkey tied as a T base, thorax of dubbed yellow rabbit fur and hackle of ginger tied parachute style, tail is a few ginger hackle fibres. Though the parachute pattern Gierach describes is given a specific purpose of imitating sulphurs it is a useful pattern for most small olive hatches when the trout are not too picky.

Sunshine

The effects of sunshine on the trout's aquatic habitat are important. Too little sun affects plant growth which in turn means less cover for trout and the invertebrates which form part of their staple diet. Too much sun means plant growth can be so great it begins to stifle the resident trout and a harmful deoxygenation of the water can occur. Trout are light-sensitive creatures and they will normally shy away from light when it goes directly into their eyes. Brilliant sun which is aligned with the direction of the current in a river or the wind in a stillwater can have the effect of blinding fish and they do not see the fly as sharply as when the sun has moved round or sunk below the horizon. Sunshine also has the effect of warming the water and as long as it is in keeping with normal local temperature fluctuations, trout benefit from this warming effect which will bring on insect hatches. Unnaturally prolonged excess of bright sun can cause trout *stress*. In hot conditions some trout will produce an extra coat of *mucous* to help keep their body temperature normal.

Suspender Flies

Suspender patterns do more or less what their name suggests, the fly hangs suspended in the surface film. Suspenders make excellent midge pupa imitations when fished on a very slow retrieve. The pattern can be made in any variety of colours (olive, green or red are popular) and the dressing is simple with a body of seal's fur, rib of fine silver wire, thorax of brown turkey fibres or peacock *herl*, tail of white fluorescent wool and head a small ball of ethafoam wrapped in nylon mesh (ladies stockings are a good material to contain the foam).

Tackle

Tackle is the all encompassing generic term for all the accoutrements and equipment anglers cart about when going fishing. The term is used on both sides of the Atlantic.

Tackle Bag

The design of tackle bags has seen a few changes from the earliest form of bag which was the *creel*. Traditionally canvas or similar would be used to make the bag with one shoulder strap so you carried the weight over one side of your body all day. Different materials came into play but the basic design of a pocketed bag remained the same through the 1900s. It wasn't until the late 1980s that tackle bag manufacturers realised the benefits to our backs of two straps rucksack style. Single strap tackle bags still have a place for boats or waters where you do not have to walk far to fish however rucksack style bags are now *de rigueur* for fishing escapades involving long walks.

Tail (of a Fly)
There is always a niggling little doubt over the efficacy of putting a fibre or wool tail on an artificial fly. Pundits who favour *wingless wonders* as general attractors of trout do not always insist on a tail, in fact in most of these patterns it is much reduced to a tag or is superfluous. Once you get down to hatch matching however it will be noticed that some natural insects do indeed have tails. *Olives* have two tails while *mayflies* (Green Drakes) have three so artificials should copy these as far as possible. Apart from a useful exact imitation, a tail on dry fly helps to give the body balance as well as assisting buoyancy. Note the tail fly of a *loch style* leader with droppers is simply the one at the end sometimes also referred to as the point fly, it may or may not have an actual tail.

Tailwater
In the US tailwater angling involves fishing on the narrow fast exit water just below a dam or some similar constriction in the flow of water. This water will be well oxygenated and can provide good habitat for trout while the rest of the river is low. The term has similar connotations to the UK's fishing the tail of a pool.

Take
The 'take' is probably the most exciting part of fly fishing for trout. It's the moment the trout seizes your fly and makes off with it clasped in its jaws. 'A feeding fish is a taking fish' is one of the most well known axioms in fly fishing. A little confusingly however if an angler talks of having a take, it can also mean that the trout rose to the fly but did not fully connect. Sometimes it is thought that a trout can be induced to take by various techniques of working the fly including raising and lowering the rod tip or speeding up the retrieve.

Taking Times
Taking times are important for the fisherman as they are the times when trout are most likely to be feeding either on or below the surface. Early and late in the season trout will generally have their taking periods during

Taking times.

the warmer parts of the day. Mid season the taking times will be more specific perhaps at dawn and dusk when there is not intense sunlight on the water. These periods of activity will vary from country to country, for example New Zealand trout are much more used to brilliant light penetrating their habitat and will still take insects from the surface whereas the *brown trout* of Scotland tend to shrink away from bright sunshine. Nevertheless anglers will always want to be *au fait* with the principal taking times of their local trout as it will increase their catch rates considerably.

Taper
In the days of *horsehair lines* the whole fly line was all tapered one way to a fine single delicate hair point. The modern polymer-coated fly line replaced this in the form of a double taper. This means the line gets skinny at both the reel end and the fly end and has the 'fatter' part in the middle. The thinner taper is supposed to assist delicate fly presentation. Double taper lines differ from *weight forward* lines which have the heavier part of the line toward the point as the name suggests.

Tapered Leader
Following on from the good old *horsehair* and *gut*, the modern nylon tapered leader copied and improved on the original design. Different strengths and thickness of nylon are knotted down to a fine point for the fly to be attached. This assists in the turnover capacity of the nylon and helps in a more delicate presentation. UK anglers will spend hours knotting different nylons together in order to create the perfect tapered leader however our American counterparts go out and buy the complete article all neatly made in a clear flexible version tapered down to a 3x point. The trouble with these fused together versions is that if you keep changing flies the skinny bit at the end is greatly reduced.

Teal Flies
In the UK there are a series of *traditional* flies known as the Teal and Green, Teal and Black, Teal and Silver and so on. Speckled teal feather seems to be particularly effective when a less solid colour of grey wing is called for. They are effective in lochs where the water is lightly peat stained or with a darker base perhaps because of this stippled barred wing. The dressing for one of the most popular versions, the Teal and Green which makes an excellent small fish *lure*, is as follows: tail GP tippet, body green seal's fur or green floss for a sparser dressing, rib narrow silver tinsel, olive hen hackle throat (optional) and teal wing. The wing can either be a bunch of fibres or rolled over. Teal is a rather brittle

feather to work with but it is worthwhile persevering as the end result makes a good trout attractor.

Terrestrials

When trout are taking 'terrestrials' it means they are feeding on land-born insects which are being blown on to the water. Noted land-born insects which trout enjoy include the *Black Gnat*, *Bibio* and the *Daddy*. The effectiveness of terrestrials in bringing on a rise is to some extent dependent on wind strength and direction. If there is no wind the trout simply cannot access the abundant food supply happening over land and will look for aquatic based feeding.

Territory

As a very general rule of thumb, *brown trout* tend to be more territorial in nature than *rainbows* as the latter follows a shoaling pattern. The bigger the brownie the larger its territory and the more stoutly it is likely to defend it. Smaller fish will compete ferociously for the best territory in their neck of the woods. Trout move up the *pecking order* as they grow larger, once a good territory is vacated it is not long until the up and coming fish moves in. A good quality territory comprises of plentiful feeding and easy access to shelter from predators.

Tight lines

A tight line means a trout has been captured on the other end and it is what most anglers strive for. Wishing each other 'Tight Lines' is a simple way of saying good luck though of course we all know in trout fishing that luck has little or nothing at all to do with it!

Tippet

Tippet is just another way of describing the fine fly end of *nylon* or *leader* you are using. Today 4lb tippet is just the same as 4lb nylon but in the old days the tippet part was the skinny end on to which the fly was attached. GP (Golden Pheasant) tippets however are feather fibres commonly used to form the tail of an artificial fly. They are normally yellow or orange in colour and have a distinctive black bar across them with a black tip.

Top of the Water Fishing

In the UK if you are fishing top of the water then you will be using a floating line and targeting the top layer down to about six feet or so. This style of angling can be done with either dry or wet flies. *Loch style* fishing is sometimes described as top of the water angling even though it involves a team of wet flies.

Top of the water fishing using traditional flies.

Traditional

In the UK if flies and/or methods are described as traditional, then they are following in well trodden footsteps. Traditional lake/loch patterns are along the lines of *Zulu*, *Invicta* or *Soldier Palmer* while traditional river flies might well include the *Greenwell's Glory*, *Black Gnat* or *Hare's Ear*. Wet flies are considered more deeply traditional than dry flies which only came into being in the mid to late 1800s. Traditional angling methods centre on the use of floating line and wet fly, see also *loch style fishing*. It is interesting that as time has gone on the term 'traditional' now encompasses a lot more of the modern, even lure fishing for stocked rainbows is described thus, a sign that we all grow older perhaps!

Treatise (Treatise of Fishing with an Angle)

The *Treatise* is one of the earliest comprehensive books written on angling with rod and line. It dates back to 1420 and it is often attributed to Dame Juliana Berners. However the book is actually a compilation of European fishing writings brought together under the one title. It is packed full of little gems of information and is the ultimate proof that there is absolutely nothing new in fishing. The *Treatise* laid down the foundations of the artificial fly detailing dressings for different months of the season. A number of these original patterns are still in use today under various renamed guises. Quotes from it are wonderfully apt and they include 'It shall be light and full nimble to fish with' which concerned the qualities of a good rod, under 'Impediments' to catching fish it describes an east wind as the worst 'for commonly neither in winter nor summer the fish will not bite then'. The best line in the *Treatise* beautifully describes the sport of angling stating that you go fishing 'for your solace, to procure the health of your body and especially, of your soul'. How true!

Trichoptera

Trichoptera are the order of flies with roof-shaped wings more commonly known as *sedge* (UK) or *caddis* (US). Occasionally in the US the term 'Trico' appears to be used for caddis flies though somewhat confusingly Trico is also used to describe flies with three colours in their make up. Natural flies of the Trichoptera Order on either side of the pond have four wings which lie in an inverted V close to the body of the insect. The wings are often mottled in colour and all have a very fine coating of hair. Trichoptera also have two long antenna but no tail. Hatches in the UK tend to reach a peak during the Summer months with the first profuse hatches occurring as early as May.

Triploid

Triploid fish are sterile and cannot reproduce. Triploid rainbows are often used in the UK to restock commercial fisheries where the need is for *put and take* fishing. These fish have largely lost the need to try and migrate to spawn however they can still go into spawning dress and become much darker in colour with crimson red flanks.

Trolling

Trolling is a method of fishing usually involving spinning gear where the rod is placed at right angles to the boat and a good length of line with spinner attached is let out behind the boat. The angler does not cast as such rather the spinner is moved by operating the engine at low revs. Effective trolling is usually done in wide arcs so that the spinner is swung round in a curve rather than dragged along in a straight line. Trolling is often not allowed on fly only waters as it is thought to disturb the trout population and disrupt normal fly fishing practice. In Scotland it is an offence to fish with a rod which is not hand held and therefore trolling treads a fine line between the legal and illegal. Trolling flies on a long line out of the back of the boat when motoring is also frowned upon.

Trophy Trout
Photographs of large trout of 5lb plus held aloft by a triumphant angler are still commonplace in some UK fishing magazines. These fish will usually be stocked rainbows which have been caught in manmade ponds or reservoirs. There is a particular culture which surrounds these type of trophy trout with a degree of competition often involved as to who gets their picture in the paper with the largest specimen. It is a matter of personal choice whether you participate or eschew this type of glory. To me a picture of a large wild brown trout being genuinely returned in order to proliferate and pass on its undoubted top quality genes says a lot more about the character of the fisherman.

Trotted
When fishing with bait (usually worm) for river trout the bait is cast upstream and then 'trotted' back. This method is done with a raised rod tip and the worm bumped back down in the current and it is an extremely productive method in skilled hands. Trotting bait is normally done in high coloured water when fly is proving ineffective. When upstream nymph fishing with heavy flies the method is very similar to trotting the whole object being to keep the nymph off the bottom and make it drift back down in a natural looking way.

Tungsten
Tungsten is a heavy metal used in the construction of weighted nymphs. Tungsten nymphs sink like a stone in deep, fast water and are used in *Czech nymphing* techniques. The metal is usually added to the fly in wire form wound round the body of the fly in different thicknesses to achieve different sink speeds.

Twitch
When a dry fly is cast out and left static on a stillwater it is often a useful ploy to give it a little twitch now and again. Twitching a dry fly on a river is not so essential as the current will give it a lifelike movement however stillwater dry fly calls for a little lateral thinking. If you have no success with a static dry then it is likely you have your fly over a dead territory with no trout lingering in the vicinity. You must therefore start some kind of retrieve but still keep the artificial looking reasonably lifelike. Twitching the fly back in a short pull followed by a static rest then another twitch imparts a fair degree of animation to the fly and a nearby trout may well decide to *take*.

A trophy trout.

United States Trout Fishing

Trout fishing in the US does not have quite the long history of the Europeans and in some ways it benefits from a lack of pretentiousness. While the British anguished over the merits of dry fly over wet, upstream nymph over downstream *traditional* at times getting extremely bogged down in *purism*, the North Americans did not appear to have such hang-ups and simply got on with enjoying fishing. Today in the US many waters are managed by the State Department which will often have a whole government run section designated to manage and conserve local fish populations and oversee local angling practices. See also *Eastern and Western Flies*.

Upwellings

In natural deep stillwaters water can stratify between a warm upper layer and a cold lower layer. This frequently happens unseen in summer but the angler may well become aware of the effect when upwellings of cold water occur. This happens when cold water replaces the warm water layer which is literally pushed offshore by high winds. Trout sometimes react to these upwellings by altering their feeding habits. In some cases they may go off the boil a bit close in as their normal range of shallow water invertebrates gets pushed out into deeper water, alternatively the cold water movement may encourage them to come in to water which was previously too warm.

Upwinged Flies

The upwinged order of flies are the Ephemeroptera and consist of the *olive* and *mayfly* groups. Upwinged flies are especially beloved by trout as they offer a good target to hit on or near the surface. Imitations of upwinged flies are legion and all phases of the insect nymph to dun and spinner are covered, as long as the shape and colour of the artificial are reasonable there is a good chance of fish taking it.

Venables (Colonel)

Famous anglers of the 1600s include Walton, Cotton and the less sung but just as wise angler Colonel Venables. Venables wrote the *Experienced Angler or Angling Improved* in 1662 and though the book is small it is full of shrewd observation and salient advice on everything from *rods* to *palmer* worms. Reading Venables' work is like seeing the past and the

United States trout fishing in spectacular surroundings.

future all in one go. Never let anyone tell you there is something new in fishing, there isn't and Venables without question proves that.

Vest

The use of a fishing vest or waistcoat has military connotations. During war time soldiers found it necessary to transport lots of smallish items on their person over rough terrain. Fishing vests have therefore grown on from this original idea. They are indispensable pieces of kit furnished with enough pockets to carry a wide range of fishing accoutrements. There are numerous waistcoat styles on the market and it is best to choose one most suited to the type of fishing you are usually doing. Commonsense dictates avoiding vests with so many pockets you look like a Michelin man if all you are doing is walking a few feet from car to river. Also try and find an appropriate 'gender vest' that is one suited to a woman's or man's physique. Speaking as a female, too many vest pockets up front are cumbersome and restrict casting!

Vice

In the earliest days of artificial fly construction, the vice did not exist. Flies were tied in hand and it took a fair amount of delicate finger work to get it right. It is likely that the use of a vice to hold the hook while manipulating the dressing first came into being in the mid nineteenth century. The principal requirement of a good vice is the tightness of the 'jaws' to hold the hook still as you wind thread and feather around it. This prerequisite might sound like plain common sense but you would be surprised how many modern manufactured metal vices still fail to meet this basic condition.

Voe

In the UK a voe is a Nordic word for a long arm of seawater which stretches inland. Voes are common to the Shetland Isles, Ireland and Norway. These inlets sometimes are also known as firths, provide sheltered harbour for boats as well as a lush habitat for fish. At the head of the voe there will usually be a river or small burn running into the sea and for many game fish this may well be their natal stream. Both sea trout and salmon use voes as comparatively safe feeding areas. The voes of Shetland were at one time world famous for their top quality sea trout angling. Extraordinary catches of large sea trout weighing 5lb plus to fly fishers were common in the first half of the twentieth century however from the 1960s catches of these big trout slowly declined perhaps due to changing conditions at sea. Also the placing of commercial *fish farms* in sheltered voes right in the path of migratory fish had disastrous consequences when sea lice on the farmed fish cross-infected wild fish causing them infinite harm. Voe fly

Japanese angler Rumiko wearing an elegant fishing vest.

A good vice is essential for fly tying.

fishing with *streamers* or *lures* is still practised in Shetland and elsewhere around the British Isles and success can still be had if you catch the tide on the two hours prior to high tide when the trout are moving in or alternatively two hours after high tide when the fish are falling back.

Waders

In the UK, prior to the invention of the rubber boot, waders were simply sturdy leather boots which the angler wore in the water until such time as he or she could not stand the cold any longer. Wading was practised as far back as the 1600s but then only sparingly indeed. *Venables* warned of the perils of sciatica and rheumatism brought on from the effects of wading in cold water. Rubber wading trousers came into being in the mid nineteenth century and the rest followed as product manufacturing got better and better. Today we have a whole range of wading boots in rubber, nylon, neoprene or breathable materials made in knee, thigh, waist or chest sizes with either stocking foot or boot foot soles. Breathable waders are essential for hot climates as anything else can bring on heat stroke. however rubber or nylon are fine for temperate regions and neoprene offers excellent protection against cold weather. Despite modern manufacturers' claims to the contrary, waders can be prone to leaks especially at the seams so buy only those that are well sealed and taped inside with as few joins in the material as possible.

Wading

Quiet, careful, stealthy wading pays dividends as you neither scare the trout nor upend yourself in cold water. Small shuffle steps are advised especially on slippery rocks and in places where you cannot see down through the water to what your feet are placed on. Giant strides make a major disturbance in the water and can lead to you stepping off a ledge into deep and dangerous water. If you are not wearing your *lifejacket*, falling in while wading can kill, usually hypothermia strikes first then drowning. It is important to wade into a water quietly as trout may be feeding close in and heavy footsteps only serve to scare them away. Wading might also not be advised near to known spawning redds as all you will do is disturb this important fish habitat.

Wading Boots

If you decide to purchase modern stocking foot waders, wading boots have to be purchased separately. The uppers of these are made of a range of

Wading the shallows.

materials including leather, synthetics, neoprene, vinyl and rubber. The sole is however the most important part. In all truth, rubber cleats and felt soles are not sufficient to stop you slipping on algae-covered rocks. If the vast majority of your fishing is done in a slip and slide environment it is definitely worth investing in boots with a studded sole. Some felt soles (which are quieter than hefty rubber) can have screw in studs added to order, alternatively you can buy rubber soled boots with studs already inserted. A good tip is to try the boots on with your intended waders as the stocking feet can add a little more bulk in the shoe and a bigger size than normal might be needed.

Wading Stick

A wading stick or staff is a prerequisite if you are wading fast, dangerous waters. A stick helps you keep your balance as you manoeuvre around unseen rocks hidden below the surface. The older you get the more interest you have in self preservation and wading sticks become *de rigueur* on any outing involving wading in reasonably deep water. Avoid a wading stick with a hard metal tip as it gives an alarming noisy clink underwater as you move along and fish may well flee from you.

Weight Forward

Modern fly lines can be manufactured to high specifications and are often made in the weight forward (WF) style. This simply means that the bulk of the thicker part of the line is to the forward section. WF lines greatly assist casting across strong wind and can give added distance if that is what is required. The only disadvantage of a weight forward is that it can give a heavier presentation and can look a might clumsy in a flat calm. See also *Double Taper*.

Western Flies

In the US western fly tying styles are somewhat more dressed up than their *Eastern* counterparts. Famous fly tyer Jack Dennis describes Western flies as ones made by 'over-hackling' the fly in order to make it more buoyant. Western *streamers* and *wet flies* are also tied in larger sizes than their eastern counterparts and any tail added is likely to be made of a firm fibre like elk or moose hair.

Wet Fly

Wet flies are the oldest designs of flies, they came on the scene in Europe many centuries before *dry fly* appeared in the mid 1800s. One of the earliest wet flies recorded is attributed to a Roman soldier Aelian of the third century AD. The pattern bears a resemblance to a *Soldier Palmer* with a body of red wool and brown cock hackle feather. In general terms, the first flies designed were fished as they fell and once a fly got a good soaking it sank below the surface and became forever known as wet fly. In the UK wet flies of the nineteenth and early twentieth century were mainly of the sparse variety sometimes little more than a twist of thread and hackle on a bare hook. *Spiders* were the ultimate in skinny, dull coloured wet flies, *fancy flies* in bright tinsels are also basically wet flies. Wet fly fishing on rivers is traditionally executed with an *across and down* cast while wet fly on stillwaters often involves *loch style* angling. Nymphs also fall into the wet fly category though today they are often classed separately from wets.

Selecting a wet fly.

Wet Fly Fishing
Wet fly technique is the oldest and the simplest method of fishing. The fly or flies (see also *Loch Style*) is cast methodically to search the water for trout. In river wet fly this will normally involve casting *across and down* thereby covering likely looking trout lies as the fly swings round in the current. With his next cast the angler will take a step downstream and repeat the process. Wet fly fishing on stillwaters is similarly methodical casting and moving along the shore as fast as you would in a drifting boat.

White Trout
Classifications of trout in the British Isles during the 1700s and 1800s make reference to 'white' trout being found along parts of the west coast of Scotland. These are now thought to be *sea trout* which were common to these shores and their small *spate* rivers.

Wickham's Fancy
This is a comparatively old UK pattern designed in the mid 1800s. Dr Wickham, a River Test angler, wanted to copy a local fly known as the Cockerton. His fly tying friend duly made the fly but unfortunately it did not resemble the Cockerton and by happy accident the Wickham's Fancy was born. Today this pattern is used in dry or wet fly situations on stillwaters or rivers with equal ease. It has vague sedge or olive connotations and with its flashy gold body and straggly hackle can also be taken as a shrimp pattern. It's a particularly useful fly for hard, bright conditions and the dressing is fairly simple; body flat gold, rib fine gold wire, palmered hackle ginger cock, tail of cock hackle fibres and wings of starling or mallard.

Wild Trout
In the UK some forward thinking fisheries scientists and managers now make an important distinction between *native trout* and wild ones. In the past this distinction was ignored or glossed over. A wild trout is therefore any trout which has spawned in a wild habitat even though its parentage may be corrupted by an introduced *brown trout* going on to spawn with a native trout. From the mid 1800s thousands of UK waters were stocked with *hatchery*-reared browns and this practice, thought at the time to be beneficial in bringing in new blood, actually contaminated important brown trout genetic lines stretching back to the last Ice Age. It could be argued that any naturally spawned trout is a wild one but there is an important conservation issue here. There are still some genetically distinct strains surviving in the UK and these native trout should therefore be conserved first. It is not good enough to say that restocking brown

Wild Trout

trout to mix with 'natives' is a protective measure for fish stocks; it isn't and the issue is far more complex and deserves proper attention by nature and environmental bodies.

Wind

The influence of wind on rivers and stillwaters is important. On flowing water strong winds may dictate which bank you fish and whether you can cast upstream or down. A light breeze however helps disguise your intentions and may improve casting distance if coming from behind. Wind direction on stillwaters has a similar effect on the bank and if fishing from a boat the wind will dictate the line of *drift*. Prolonged gales can pile up warm water at one end of a stillwater (see also *upwellings*) and this can have a detrimental effect on the fishing. In the past wind direction was given considerable credence with rhymes devised over the merits of a south or west wind (warmer and better) or a northerly or easterly (colder and not so productive). Anglers pay slightly less attention to these old sayings now but there is still a general belief that a steady wind from one direction is better than one which switches through 360 degrees in as many minutes. Wind will also affect your ability to cast accurately especially if you are trying to cast into or across a gale. Lighter breezes can be coped with a *weight forward line*.

Wind Lanes

On stillwaters, wind lanes fall into two different categories. The first are those obvious white lines of foam which form distinct streaks downwind during a strong wind. These lines contain extra oxygen bubbles as well as small food items trapped in their drift. Trout will often lie in or next to these wind lanes and when the bounty they bear is particularly rich, the fish will swim upwind gulping down nymphs or spent insects as they go. The second type of wind lane is less obvious and occurs during periods of calm interspersed with a light breeze. Slicks of warm water are gently wafted across the colder surface layer and these look slightly oily in nature compared to the rest of the water. Trout love these slicks as the warmer water temperature holds more lush feeding especially in a cool climate water such as the lochs of northern Scotland.

Window

The shape of a trout's eye dictates how it sees things through a partly triangular window extending from its head and up toward the water surface. Vision is excellent within this window but there are blind spots. Anglers should exploit the blind areas to gain the best chance of creeping up on the trout unseen. See also *Eyesight in Trout*. There are other connotations to this term however and anglers will often refer to a weather window. This means a period in the day in early or late season when the storm/gale/rain abates and a little glimpse of sun might appear. Weather windows bring a short warming change in temperature and it is imperative that you have a line in the water when these are going on. A hatch will usually occur during a window and trout are spurred into action, you must be too!

Winged Flies

Some of the earliest winged flies date back to the *Treatise* where the patterns described have wings made principally of partridge or mallard though feathers from the buzzard or jay were also used. The purposes of wings may have been to give the fly an insect shape but in the olden days wings also gave the fly a more aerodynamic quality being caught by the wind and blown forward on to the water. Rolled wings are usually found on wet flies and are one bunch of feather fibres rolled over and tied in at the head of the hook and then sloped back toward the hook bend. If the wings stand prominently out from the hook they are known as *Clyde style flies*. Split wings used in dry fly angling are also tied in at the head of the fly but use two separate slips of fibres tied to stand upright. Advanced wings simply take the feather split wing one step further and cock the separate wing feathers toward the eye of the hook making them highly prominent. *Hair wing* trout flies are a comparatively new invention and are popular in US designs for example elk or bucktail hair wing.

Wingless Wonders
This is a UK colloquialism used to describe flies like the *Soldier Palmer*, *Zulu* or the *Bumble* range. It simply means these are top quality fly patterns made without the addition of a wing.

Wooly Worm (USA Spelling)
The Wooly Worm is a well known and highly versatile pattern in common use throughout the US. It's a very simple palmered wet fly tied in sizes 8 to 16, weighted or un-weighted and in any combinations of colour you care to consider. Noted fly tyer Jack Dennis recommends black, peacock herl or dark brown bodies with either badger, grizzly, black or brown hackle. I'd like to think there is a way back connection to the British *palmer* worm of the 1600s but this may a little fanciful. The dressing is very easy with chenille body in any of the aforementioned colours, a tail of red or yellow floss and an appropriately coloured palmered hackle which is not too dense. It looks a bit like a shrimp but can be taken as a caddis or a nymph as well. In the UK there is a version called the Worm Fly which has similar basic colours and design but the hackle is not palmered.

Work/Working
In the UK working the fly is the important part when you impart some life to it moving it back toward you on a retrieve. It is essential to keep good contact with the fly, failure to do so will result in you fumbling with loose line and being unable to work the fly properly. In the US the fly is not so much worked as the trout. A trout 'working' in the shallows means the fish is busy feeding on a choice bit of lunch be that insect or crustacean. Working trout will nearly always have a go at your fly as long as you don't spook them first.

Wulff
Famous US angler Lee Wulff designed his range of Wulff patterns back in the 1930s but they remain everlasting favourites with those who like their dry flies a little beefy rather than super sparse. They feature high floating durable materials like bucktail and are excellent trout attractors when big olive, mayfly and/or sedge are on the water. Wulffs can be used on flowing or stillwater with equal ease and are great all-rounders. These patterns

Wulff.

come in a variety of colours notably Grey, White or Royal Wulffs in sizes 8 to 14. *Purist* they ain't but who cares if they catch fish! The dressing for the Grey Wulff is as follows: head hackle blue dun cock, wing brown bucktail tied upright or split in a V shape, body grey rabbit or angora wool and a tail of bucktail fibres.

Yellow Sally

Though fly tyers will often incorporate yellow into a dressing there are actually very few insects in the UK which are bright yellow in colour. The Yellow Sally, a member of the flat winged *stonefly* family, is the most recognised one and these medium-sized insects are common throughout the UK preferring a stony-based habitat. Exact imitations are not extremely necessary just something with a flash of gold and olive in it such as the *Wickham's Fancy*. The Yellow May pattern is also a useful replica even though this pattern was meant originally for *olive* imitations.

Zulu

It is appropriate that this compendium ends with one of the oldest designs of flies found in the UK. Its origins descend from the first *palmer* flies of the twelfth century and then reappear as a variant of a Cotton fly of the 1600s. It is thought the fly had another name prior to its current one and that Zulu was only attached to it after the British 'Zulu wars' in Africa in the nineteenth century. The fly can be made in at least three types, Black, Blue and Gold but there also glitzy twenty-first century models with sparkly materials added. The nearest equivalent in US fly making is the *Woolly Worm*. This is a lake/loch fly *wingless wonder* par excellence. It is best used as a top *dropper* when you have a slim line *lure* on the tail fly, however it is equally effective as a point fly when the trout are not too fussy. The Zulu's essential attraction to trout are its colours of black, red and silver, it is not an exact imitation of anything but boy, does it catch fish! The Black Zulu is dressed as follows: body black wool or seal's fur, rib fine silver tinsel, tail red wool and black palmered hen hackle. On its day there are few more productive stillwater flies than the Zulu in either in its Black or Blue dress.

A huge trout well hooked on the Zulu.

SELECT BIBLIOGRAPHY

J Buckland, *The Fisherman's Companion*, Country Life

G Bucknall, *The Bright Stream of Memory*, Swan Hill Press

A Courtney Williams, *A Dictionary of Trout Flies*, A & C Black

J Dennis, *Western Trout Fly Tying Manual*, Snake River Books

Frost and Brown, *The Trout*, Collins

J Gierach, *Good Flies*, Lyons Press

Maitland and Campbell, *Freshwater Fishes*, HarperCollins

C B McCully, *A Dictionary of Fly Fishing*, Oxford University Press

T Stewart, *Two Hundred Popular Flies*, A & C Black

Stolz and Schnell (editors), *The Wildlife Series – Trout*, Stackpole Books

J Waller Hills, *A History of Fly Fishing for Trout*, B Shurlock

INDEX

A

Abundance Factor 11
Ace of Spades 11
Acid rain 11
Acid water 11
Across and down 12
Action (fish) 12
Action (rod) 13
Adams 13
Adaptation 13
Aerialise 14
Aerial Route 14
AFTM 14
Agile Darter 14
Age of trout 14
Aggression 14
Alder fly 17
Algae 17
Alkaline water 17
Ally's Shrimp 18
Amadou 19
Anchor Ice 19
Angler's Curse 19
Angling 20
Apache trout 20
Arbor 21
Arctic Charr 22
Artificial 22

B

Back end fishing 23
Backing 23
Backing up 23
Baggot 24
Bag Limit 24
Balance 24
Bank fishing 24
Barbless hooks 26
Barometric pressure 26
Basket 26
Bass 27
Beaching trout 27
Beads 27
Beat 27
Beetles 28
Behaviour (in trout) 28
Bibio 29
Biot 29
Bi-visible flies 29
Black Flies 29
Black Fly 30

Black Gnat 30
Black Trout 30
Blae 31
Blank 31
Bloodworm 31
Boat fishing 31
Bobber float 32
Bob fly 33
Boil 33
Bolognese rods 33
Brackish water 33
Braided leaders 35
Braided loops 35
Breaking strain BS 35
Breeding trout 36
Brook trout 36
Browns, Brownies,
    Brown Trout 37
Bugs 38
Bull trout 38
Bumbles 38
Buoyancy aids 39
Butcher 40
Butt 40
Buzzer 40

C

Caddis 41
Cane rods 41
Cannibal trout 41
Capes 42
Cast 42
Casting a fly 42
Catch and release 44
Catch return 44
Cat's Whisker 45
Caution in trout 45
Characteristics
    (browns) 45
Children fishing 45
Chironomids 47
Claret 47
Climate change 47
Clouds 48
Clouser 49
Clunker 49
Clyde style flies 49
Coch Y Bondhu 50
Colouration 50
Competition amongst
    trout 52

Competition angling 52
Concealment 52
Condition of trout 52
Conditions 53
Cormorants 53
Cowdung fly 53
Crawdads 53
Creek 54
Creel 54
Cruising fish 54
Crustaceans 54
Cul de Canard (CDC) 55
Current 56
Cute factor 56
Cutthroat trout 56
Czech Nymphs 57

D

Daddies 57
Dams 57
Damsel flies 58
Dance 59
Daphnia 59
Dapping 59
Dark Olive 60
Deer hair 60
Dibble 61
Disc 62
Distance 63
Distribution (of trout) 63
Double hander 63
Double haul 64
Doubles (wee) 64
Dour 64
Drag 65
Drake(s) 65
Dressing 65
Drift 66
Drogue 67
Droppers 67
Dry fly 67
Dubbing 68
Duck Fly 68
Dunkeld 68
Duns 69

E

Early fishing 69
Ears (in trout) 69
Eastern flies 70
Educated trout 70

Effort	70	Grasshopper	90	Ke He	109
Eggs (imitation)	71	Gravel	91	Keep net	109
Eggs of trout	71	Gravid	91	Kelts	110
Elasticity	71	Grayling	91	Kill	110
Elk hair	72	Green midge	91	Klinkhamer flies	110
Emerging insects	72	Greenback trout	92	Knots	110
Ephemera	72	Green Peter	92	Kype	110
Eutrophication	72	Greenwell's Glory	92		
Evening fishing	73	Grip	92	L	
Eyesight (trout)	73	Grouse wing flies	93	Lake trout	111
		Growth (of trout)	94	Landing nets	112
F		Gut	94	Large Dark Olive	112
Fancy Flies	74			Larvae	112
Feeding	74	H		Lateral line (fish)	112
Feeding fish	75	Habitats	94	Leader	114
Felt soles (waders)	75	Hackle	95	Leven trout	114
Ferox trout	75	Hairwing flies	95	Lie(s)	114
Fingering	77	Halcyon days	95	Life history (trout)	115
Fingerling trout	77	Hands	96	Lifejacket	115
Finnock	77	Hard water	97	Lifespan	115
Finning fish	77	Hare's Ear	97	Light (effects on trout)	115
Fins	78	Hatch	97	Limestone	117
Fish farming	78	Hatchery	97	Lines	117
Flash	79	Hatchery-bred trout	98	Lined (fish)	117
Flavilinea	79	Hats	98	Lochs	118
Flexible fishing	79	Head (of fly)	98	Loch Ordie	118
Flies	80	Heather fly	99	Loch Style	118
Float tubes	81	Height of water	99	Loop	118
Floating line	81	Hippers	99	Lure	120
Fluorescent materials	82	Hi Vis flies	99		
Fluorocarbon	82	Hook a trout	100	M	
Fly box	82	Hooks	100	Machair	120
Fly tying	82	Hoops	100	Management of trout	120
Food chains	83	Hoppers	101	Marabou	122
Foul hook	83	Horsehair lines	102	Marbled sedge	122
Free hand	83	Hump backed trout	102	Marbled trout	122
Freestone	83	Humpy	102	March Brown	122
Frogs	85			Marl	124
Frosts	85	I		Match the Hatch	124
Fry (trout)	85	Ice	103	Mayflies (American)	124
Frying pan hackle	87	Imitation	104	Mayfly (UK)	124
		Induce a take	104	Memory	125
G		Inspiration	104	Mend line	126
Gadger	87	Intermediate line	104	Micro patterns	126
Garden fly	87	Introducing fish	104	Midges	126
Generic flies	87	Invertebrates	106	Migration	126
Genes	88	Invicta	106	Migratory trout	127
Ghost Tip	88	Iron Blue	106	Minnows	127
Gila trout	88			Molluscs	127
Gillaroo trout	88	J		Monofilament	128
Gillie	89	Jackets	106	Movement (of prey)	128
Gills	89	Jersey Herd	108	Mucous	128
Glitter	89	Jump	108	Muddlers	128
Globugs	89	Jungle Cock	108		
Golden Olive Bumble	90			N	
Golden trout	90	K		Native trout	129
Goldheads	90	Kate McLaren	109	Natural(s)	130

Needle fly	130	Rollocks	149	Teal flies	168
No-see-ums	130	Run	149	Terrestrials	169
Nose	130			Territory	169
Nylon	131	**S**		Tight lines	169
Nymph fishing (rivers)	131	Saltwater trout fishing	150	Tippet	169
		Sandeels	150	Top of the water fishing	169
Nymph fishing (stillwater)	131	Scissors	150		
		Scuds	151	Traditional	170
Nymphs (artificial)	132	Sea trout	151	*Treatise*	170
Nymphs (natural)	132	Seals	151	Trichoptera	171
		Season	153	Triploid	171
O		Sedge	153	Trolling	171
Oak fly	133	Shrimp (artificial)	154	Trophy trout	172
Olives	133	Shrimps (natural)	154	Trotted	172
Orange	133	Sight indicator	154	Tungsten	172
Overhead cast	134	Sink tip	155	Twitch	172
Oxygen	135	Sinking line	155		
		Skunked	156	**U**	
P		Slob trout	156	United States trout fishing	174
Palmer	135	Smolt	156		
Parachute	136	Smuts	156	Upwellings	174
Parr	136	Snails (freshwater)	156	Upwinged flies	174
Parr marked trout	136	Snake roll cast	157		
Peacock herl	137	Snowfly	158	**V**	
Pecking order	137	Soldier Palmer	158	Venables, Colonel	174
Pheasant tail nymph	138	Sonaghen	158	Vest	176
Plankton	139	Spate	159	Vice (fly tying)	176
Play	139	Spawning	159	Voe	176
Pocket water	139	Spey cast	159		
Pollution	140	Spiders	159	**W**	
Predators	140	Spinner	161	Waders	179
Presentation	141	Station	161	Wading	179
Priest	141	Steelhead	161	Wading boots	179
Punkie	141	Stickleback	161	Wading stick	181
Purist/purism	141	Stillwater(s)	162	Weight forward (WF)	181
Put and take	142	Stimulator	162	Western flies	181
		Stocking	162	Wet fly	181
Q		Stocked trout	162	Wet fly fishing	183
Quill	142	Stoneflies	163	White trout	183
Quotations	142	Strap	163	Wickham's Fancy	183
		Streamers	163	Wild trout	183
R		Stress (in trout)	164	Wind	184
Rainbow trout	143	Strike	164	Wind lanes	185
Rainfall	144	Strip	164	Window	185
Reach cast	144	Sulphur	164	Winged flies	185
Red (in flies)	145	Sunshine	165	Wingless wonders	186
Redds	145	Suspender flies	165	Wooly Worm	186
Reel	146			Work/working	186
Renegade	146	**T**		Wulff	186
Reservoirs	146	Tackle	165		
Resting trout	146	Tackle bag	165	**Y**	
Retrieve	147	Tail (of a fly)	166	Yellow Sally	187
Rise	147	Tailwater	166		
Rise forms	147	Take	166	**Z**	
River trout	148	Taking times	166	Zulu	188
Rods	148	Taper	168		
Roll cast	149	Tapered leader	168		